PHILIP'S

ATLAS OF STARS AND PLANETS

AN EXPLORER'S GUIDE TO THE UNIVERSE

IAN RIDPATH

Endpapers: *Horsehead Nebula (front) and Veil Nebula (back)*.

Previous page: *the Solar System (see also pages 4–5)*.

This page: Jupiter's largest moons, Io, Europa, Ganymede and Callisto (see also pages 34–35).

First published in Great Britain in 1992
by Philip's, a division of Octopus Publishing Group Limited,
2–4 Heron Quays, London E14 4JP

Copyright © 1992, 1997, 2001, 2004 Philip's
Second edition 1997
Third edition 2001
Fourth edition 2004
Reprinted 2005

A CIP catalogue record for this book is available from the
British Library.

ISBN 0–540–08610–X

Printed in China

Details of other Philip's titles and services can be found on
our website at: www.philips-maps.co.uk

CONTENTS

THE SOLAR SYSTEM

OUR HOME in space is a planet we call the Earth. It is one of nine planets that go around the Sun, which is a star. The Earth is the third planet from the Sun. Each planet is a world in its own right, with its own surface features and conditions. For example, the biggest planets – Jupiter, Saturn, Uranus and Neptune – are not solid, but are balls of liquid and gas on which it would be impossible to land a spaceship.

The path of one body around another in space is called its *orbit*, and the time taken for the Earth to go all the way around its orbit is one year. The planets that are closest to the Sun move around their orbits more quickly than those farther away. For example, Mercury, the innermost planet, speeds around the Sun once every 3 months, while distant Pluto takes nearly 250 of our years to complete its own 'year'. You would never live long enough to reach your first birthday on either Neptune or Pluto. Together, the Sun and all the objects that orbit it make up the Solar System.

As well as moving along their orbits, the planets spin. The Earth spins once every 24 hours, which we call a day. Some other planets spin more quickly than the Earth, whereas others spin more slowly. The Earth has a smaller companion, the Moon, going around it. Most planets have at least one moon, and the giant planets have dozens. Only Mercury and Venus, the two planets closest to the Sun, are moonless.

The orbits of the planets around the Sun are almost circular, except for Pluto's. For most of the time Pluto is the most distant planet from the Sun, but part of its orbit brings it closer to the Sun than its neighbour planet Neptune – this last happened between 1979 and 1999. Fortunately, Pluto

and Neptune will never collide because their two orbits are tilted in such a way that they do not meet.

In addition to the nine planets, there is a lot of debris in the Solar System. Look in the picture for a band of rubble called the *asteroids* between the planets Mars and Jupiter. Other small, frozen bodies called *comets* move on highly elongated paths. When they come close to the Sun they heat up and grow long, flowing tails. Comets come from a swarm of icy bodies beyond the orbit of Pluto.

Asteroids

Jupiter

Neptune

▼ **Here the distances** of the planets from the Sun are shown to scale. Look how 'bunched up' the inner planets are, compared with the outer planets. But the distances between them are still enormous.

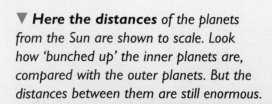

Sun   Mercury Venus Earth Mars   Asteroids   Jupiter   Saturn   Uranus

Other solar systems?

Astronomers are now able to detect planets around other stars. All the planets found so far are large, like Jupiter, but smaller planets like Earth may also exist. This artist's impression (right) shows an imaginary view from above the moon of a giant planet in another solar system. Some of the planets around other stars might have living things on them, but we cannot yet be sure.

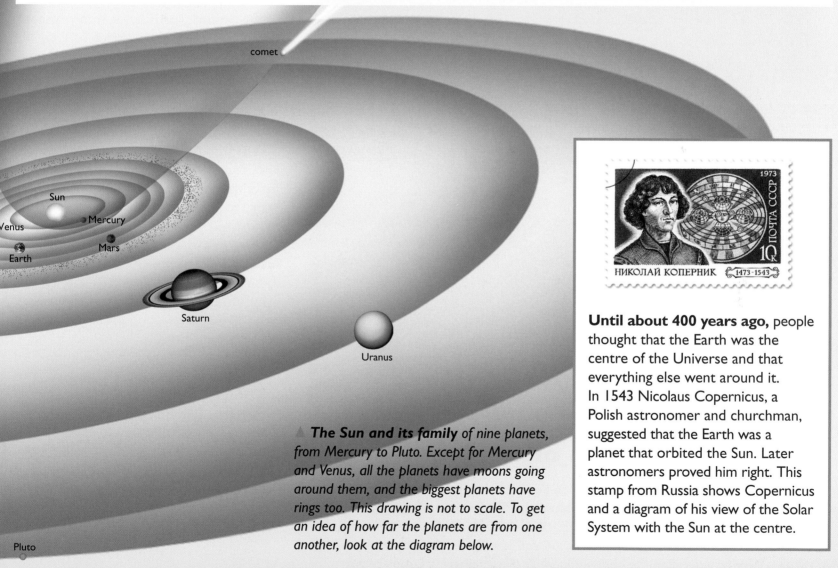

comet

Sun

Venus

Mercury

Earth

Mars

Saturn

Uranus

Pluto

The Sun and its family of nine planets, from Mercury to Pluto. Except for Mercury and Venus, all the planets have moons going around them, and the biggest planets have rings too. This drawing is not to scale. To get an idea of how far the planets are from one another, look at the diagram below.

Until about 400 years ago, people thought that the Earth was the centre of the Universe and that everything else went around it. In 1543 Nicolaus Copernicus, a Polish astronomer and churchman, suggested that the Earth was a planet that orbited the Sun. Later astronomers proved him right. This stamp from Russia shows Copernicus and a diagram of his view of the Solar System with the Sun at the centre.

Neptune

Pluto

THE SUN

EVERY MORNING the Sun rises in the east, bringing a new day. Ancient peoples regarded the Sun as a god, but we know that it is actually a star, a blazing ball of gas that gives out light and heat, which planets do not. Without the light and warmth from the Sun, there would be no life on Earth.

The Sun is huge: approximately 1.4 million kilometres (865,000 miles) wide. More than 100 Earths would be needed to stretch in a line from one side of the Sun to the other. Yet, as stars go, the Sun is only average in size and brightness.

The Sun looks much bigger and brighter than the stars we see at night because it is so much closer. Even so, the Sun is still 150 million kilometres (93 million miles) from the Earth. This is just as well for us, because its surface is a sizzling 5500°C. We would be roasted to death if we went too close. At the core of the Sun the temperature increases to an incredible 15 million degrees.

What keeps the Sun glowing? Until about 1940, this was a mystery. The Sun cannot burn like a lump of coal, for there is no air in space to feed the flames, and in any case it would have burned out long ago. One clue is that the Sun is composed entirely of gas – mostly hydrogen, the lightest gas known, plus some helium.

During the 1930s, scientists came to realize that the Sun is an enormous nuclear reactor. Inside, hydrogen is turned into helium by a process known as *fusion*. What happens is that atoms of hydrogen are crushed together (fused) by the enormous temperatures and pressures at the Sun's core, creating atoms of helium. In this process, energy is given out and this energy makes the Sun hot.

Every second, 600 million tonnes of hydrogen is turned into helium. But the Sun is so big that it has enough hydrogen left to carry on burning for thousands of millions of years – and it is already 4600 million years old. There is no danger of the Sun going out for a long while yet.

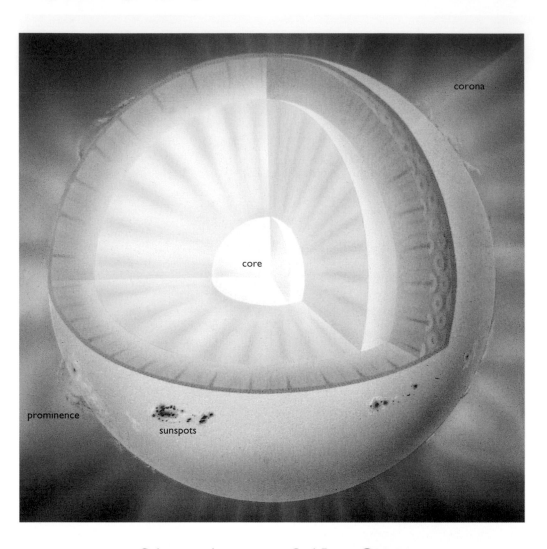

Structure of the Sun

Energy is released at the centre of the Sun. It makes its way to the surface, where it is radiated into space as heat and light. The surface of the Sun is called the *photosphere* ('sphere of light'). On it are dark markings known as *sunspots*, actually patches of cooler gas, which come and go. Above the photosphere is a thinner layer of gas called the *chromosphere* ('colour sphere'). Loops of gas termed *prominences* jut into space from the Sun's surface. Around the Sun is the *corona*, a faint halo of gas which can be seen only at total eclipses. A stream of atomic particles from the Sun known as the *solar wind* blows outwards past the planets. Occasionally, the Sun throws off huge bubbles of gas called *coronal mass ejections* which create surges in the solar wind.

SUN DATA	
DIAMETER:	1.4 million km
MASS:	333,000 × Earth
VOLUME:	1.3 million × Earth
AVERAGE DENSITY:	1.4 × water
TIME TO SPIN ON AXIS:	25.4 days (average)
DISTANCE FROM EARTH:	150 million km

Warning!

Never look at the Sun through binoculars or a telescope, for you will be blinded by its heat and light. Even staring at the Sun for more than the briefest moment is dangerous.

◀ **At sunrise and sunset,** the Earth's atmosphere makes the Sun look redder. Sometimes, as here, a fiery shaft of light called a Sun pillar can be seen extending upwards from the Sun. This effect is caused by sunlight reflecting off ice crystals high in the atmosphere.

Energy inside the Sun

In the fusion process that powers the Sun and other stars, four atoms of hydrogen are crushed together to make one atom of helium. Energy is released in the reaction (see diagrams at right). Scientists are working to harness the energy of fusion for power stations on Earth. But it is a difficult job because the process needs extremely high temperatures and pressures to work.

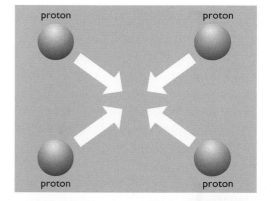

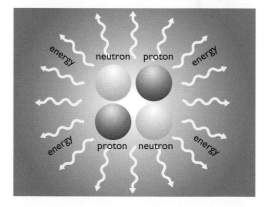

◀ **Inside the Joint European Torus,** an experimental nuclear reactor in which scientists have recreated the same fusion processes that power the Sun. This is the first step towards fusion power stations here on Earth. The right hand side of this split image shows the glowing nuclear fusion reactions in operation.

FEATURES OF THE SUN

The Sun's boiling surface is marked by dark patches called sunspots, which are actually areas of cooler gas. By everyday standards they are still very hot – even the coolest part, in the centre, is at a temperature of about 4000°C. They appear dark by contrast with the brighter surface around them, which is 1500°C hotter.

Sunspots occur where intense magnetic fields, thousands of times stronger than the magnetic field of the Earth, burst through the Sun's surface, affecting the outward flow of heat. Sunspots are only temporary, lasting from a few days to a few weeks before fading out. The number of spots visible at a time rises and falls in a cycle lasting about 11 years. Even now, no one fully understands the reason for the sunspot cycle, although it is known to be linked to changes in the Sun's magnetic field.

A typical sunspot is many times larger than the Earth. Spots often occur in groups, and some groups can stretch for 100,000 kilometres (60,000 miles) or more, a quarter of the distance from

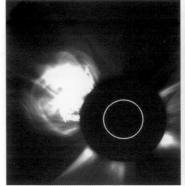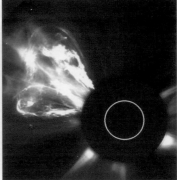

the Earth to the Moon. As the Sun rotates, the spots pass across the Sun's face from west to east. By watching sunspots, astronomers can see that the Sun rotates fastest at the equator, once every three and a half weeks, but more slowly towards the poles.

From time to time huge explosions called *flares* occur in the twisted magnetic fields above sunspots. In a few minutes, a flare releases as much energy as millions of hydrogen bombs, and fires atomic particles into space at high speeds.

Even more remarkable are immense bubbles of gas thrown off by the Sun over the course of several hours. These

▲ **A huge bubble of gas** called a coronal mass ejection (CME) blasts away from the Sun over a period of two hours as seen by the Solar and Heliospheric Observatory (SOHO) spacecraft. In this three-part sequence, the brilliant Sun is covered by a disk so that its fainter surroundings can be seen. The outline of the Sun is shown by the white circle. Bright rays emerging from behind the disk are part of the Sun's corona.

are termed *coronal mass ejections*, or CMEs for short, and can be studied only from space. Some CMEs occur at the same time as flares, but most do not. When atomic particles from flares and CMEs reach the Earth they bombard the upper atmosphere and cause a colourful night-time glow known as an *aurora* (plural *aurorae*).

Other features are clouds of gas known as *prominences*. They extend tens of thousands of kilometres into space and are often shaped like arches, because they follow looping lines of magnetism. Some prominences consist of matter being sprayed out by flares, or falling back after a flare has

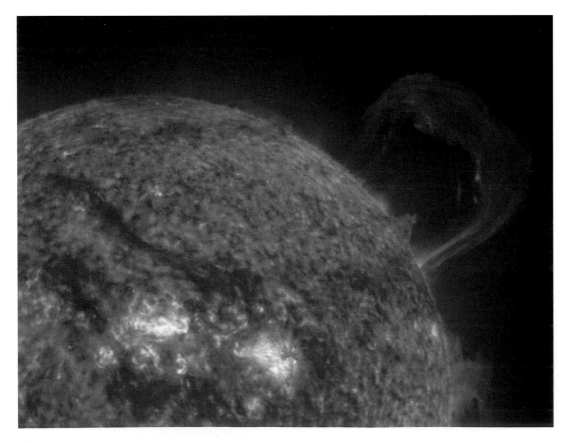

◀ **A cloud of gas** called a prominence arches into space at the edge of the Sun, photographed by the Sun-watching spacecraft SOHO. Prominences are huge clouds of relatively cool, dense gas suspended in the Sun's corona. In this picture, the hottest areas of the Sun appear white, while the coolest areas are the reddest. The image was taken at ultraviolet wavelengths, and shows up features that are invisible to the eye.

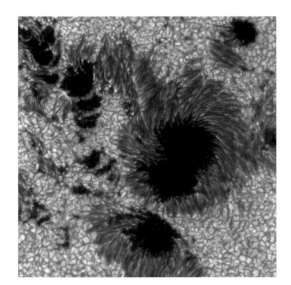

▲ **Sunspots seen in close-up**. The dark central part of a sunspot is called the umbra, *and the streaked outer part is the* penumbra. *The mottled appearance of the surroundings, termed* granulation, *is caused by rising currents of hot gas.*

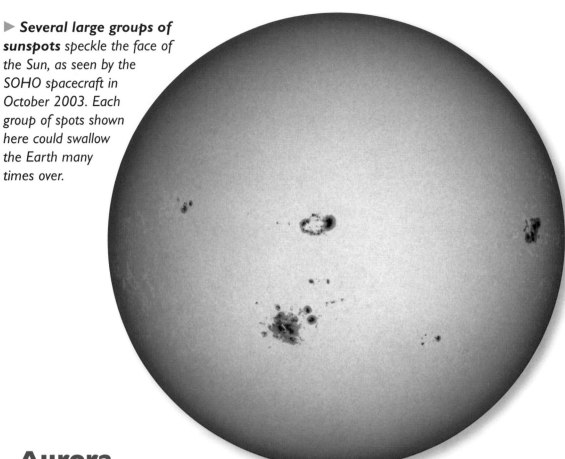

▶ **Several large groups of sunspots** *speckle the face of the Sun, as seen by the SOHO spacecraft in October 2003. Each group of spots shown here could swallow the Earth many times over.*

A space probe *called Ulysses, launched in 1990 by the European Space Agency to study the Sun, is shown on this stamp from Hungary. Ulysses flew over the north and south poles of the Sun, studying it from directions not seen from Earth.*

died away. Prominences can last for days or weeks.

In all, the Sun is a complex, ever-changing body. It is important for us to study the Sun's activity so that we can understand its effects on Earth, including changes in the Earth's climate.

Aurora

An aurora is a colourful glow high in the Earth's atmosphere caused by atomic particles from the Sun. This aurora, rising to 250 kilometres (150 miles) above the Earth, was photographed from orbit by astronauts aboard the Space Shuttle *Endeavour* in 2002. In this picture the Earth is at the bottom while stars are visible above. The red and green colours are caused by glowing atoms of oxygen. Aurorae are most often seen near the Earth's magnetic poles but sometimes, following a big flare or coronal mass ejection on the Sun, they can be seen as far south as the Mediterranean or the southern United States.

PLANET EARTH

FROM OUT in space, our home planet looks like a blue-and-white marble. The blue is the oceans while the white parts are clouds in the planet's dense atmosphere. Three-quarters of our planet is covered with water, and the Earth is the only planet in the Solar System with lots of it.

Water and an atmosphere are two reasons why there is life on Earth. Another important factor is that the Earth's distance from the Sun, 150 million kilometres (93 million miles), is just right. If it were closer to the Sun it would be too hot for life, as is Venus. Farther away, it would be too cold, like Mars.

The Earth's crust is cracked into pieces, like a damaged eggshell. These pieces are moving slowly, and volcanoes erupt along the cracks. In the past, the Earth had many more volcanoes than today. Most of our atmosphere and water is thought to have been given out by ancient volcanoes, although some may have come from comets that hit the Earth.

The atmosphere is mostly nitrogen, plus about one-fifth oxygen, which is the gas our bodies take in when we breathe. The oxygen is released by plants that

break down carbon dioxide. A form of oxygen called *ozone* protects the Earth from the Sun's dangerous ultraviolet light. But satellites in orbit around the Earth have found evidence that this ozone layer is thinning out because of man-made chemicals that have been released into the atmosphere. Action has now been taken to restrict use of the chemicals that harm the ozone layer.

▲ **Earthrise over the Moon,** *photographed by the Apollo 11 astronauts as they orbited the Moon in 1969. If you lived on the Moon, you would see the Earth pass though a cycle of phases like the phases of the Moon seen from Earth.*

Satellites keep watch on the Earth's atmosphere and oceans, measuring temperatures, wind speeds, moisture content and ocean currents. Scientists use such measurements to predict the weather and to see if the climate is changing. Other satellites survey the Earth's land surface and the things that live and grow on it.

The Earth has one moon, which is one-quarter its size. This is larger in comparison with the planet than any moon except the one orbiting tiny Pluto. In a way, therefore, the Earth and Moon are like a double planet.

◄ **Sunset seen from above** *the Earth's atmosphere by astronauts aboard the Space Shuttle. Visible to the right of the setting Sun are the dark tops of thunderclouds.*

EARTH DATA

DISTANCE FROM SUN:	150 million km
DIAMETER:	12,756 km (at the equator)
TIME TO ORBIT SUN:	365.25 days
TIME TO SPIN ON AXIS:	24 hr
AVERAGE DENSITY:	5.5 × water
TILT OF AXIS:	23.4°
NUMBER OF MOONS:	1

▶ *The Earth from space* is like a multi-coloured marble, with blue oceans, green and brown continents, and white clouds, snow and ice. This image of the western hemisphere, from the Pacific Ocean at left to the Atlantic at right and with the Arctic ice cap at top, is a combination of observations made by several satellites.

▼ *Hurricane Claudette* swirling over the Gulf of Mexico in July 2003. Photographs like this one taken from the International Space Station are important to scientists studying the Earth's weather.

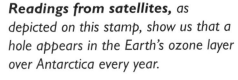

Readings from satellites, as depicted on this stamp, show us that a hole appears in the Earth's ozone layer over Antarctica every year.

TIME AND THE EARTH

We do not normally notice it, but the Earth is continuously on the move. Every year it goes once around the Sun, a journey of nearly 1000 million kilometres (600 million miles), at a speed of over 100,000 kilometres (60,000 miles) per hour. The journey takes just over 365 days, and our calendar is based on it.

As the Earth moves around its orbit, the Sun appears to change position against the background stars. The Sun traces out a yearly path around the sky, called the *ecliptic*, which is marked on the star maps on pages 54–57. The ecliptic is tilted at about 23½° to the equator as a result of the 23½° tilt of the Earth's axis. In prehistoric times, people built stone circles such as the one at Stonehenge in England to track the changing position of the Sun throughout the year. Such stone circles were the first calendars.

As well as moving along its orbit, the Earth also spins on its axis, turning once every day. This slow spin makes the Sun rise and set, and the stars cross the sky at night. Our time system is based on the daily movement of the Sun and stars. Astronomers still make accurate observations of the movement of the stars, to keep our clocks in step with the rotation of the Earth.

The Earth's day, the time it takes to spin once on its axis, is just under 24 hours. But the tides are gradually slowing down the Earth's spin and making the day longer – 200 million years from now, the day will be 25 hours long.

◀ **As the Earth turns,** the stars appear to move across the sky. In this time-exposure photograph, the star images are drawn out into curved trails around the north pole of the sky. The bright, short trail near the centre is Polaris, the north pole star. Polaris does not lie exactly at the pole of the sky — if it did, it would not leave a trail.

▶ **Time Zones:** *Because the Sun rises and sets at different times around the globe, the Earth is divided into 24 time zones, which are shown on this map. Countries in each zone keep time an exact number of hours (or sometimes half hours) different from Greenwich Mean Time. The International Date Line is an imaginary line in the Pacific Ocean where the date changes. Places to the west of the line are one day ahead of those to the east.*

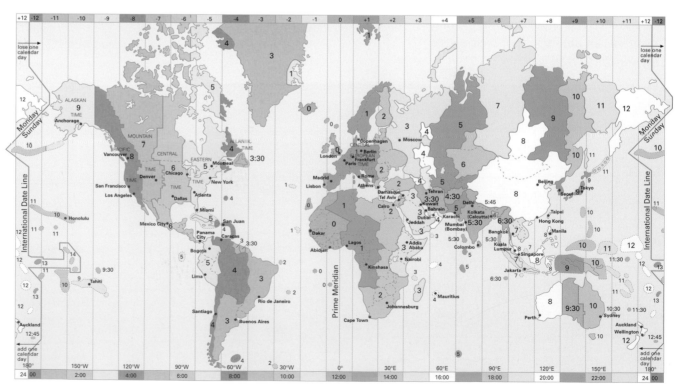

Greenwich Mean Time (GMT) *is used as a time standard worldwide. It is time as measured on the Greenwich meridian, the 0° line of longitude, which passes through the Greenwich Observatory in London. The 0° line is shown in red on this stamp, issued in 1984 to commemorate the 100th anniversary of the Greenwich meridian.*

◀ **Midsummer sunrise** *at Stonehenge, on Salisbury Plain in southern England. This stone structure dates back 4000 years, and was used to observe the times and positions of sunrise throughout the year. Stone circles like that at Stonehenge were the first observatories.*

The four seasons

There are seasons because the Earth's axis is tilted with respect to the Sun. At the *June solstice*, the Earth's north pole leans towards the Sun and days in the northern hemisphere are longest. Within the *Arctic Circle*, the Sun never sets. Six months later, at the *December solstice*, the situation is reversed. In between, at the March and September *equinoxes*, the Sun lies on the celestial equator and day and night are roughly equal the world over.

▲ **This series of exposures** *of the Sun was taken in mid-summer from Fairbanks, Alaska. Fairbanks is inside the Arctic Circle so, although it is midnight, the Sun is still visible because the Sun never sets in summer. In winter, the Sun never rises.*

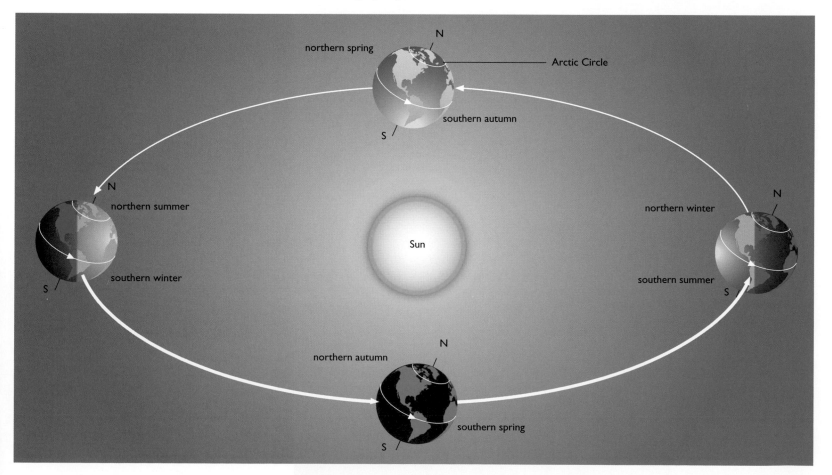

northern spring

Arctic Circle

southern autumn

northern summer

southern winter

Sun

northern winter

southern summer

northern autumn

southern spring

THE EARTH AT NIGHT

Surprisingly, signs of life on Earth are easier to see at night than by day. This remarkable view of the Earth at night was put together from photographs taken by weather satellites. The bright areas are all man-made lights, mostly from streets and buildings, so they highlight the developed areas of the world.

All of the light shown in this picture, and the energy used to create it, is wasted – it is shining upwards into space. Astronomers call this *light pollution*, and it makes the night sky brighter so that stars are difficult to see.

Look, for example, at the north-eastern United States, western Europe, and Japan. In North America, Europe and Japan, one-quarter of the world's people use about three-quarters of the world's electricity. Contrast these intensely lit areas of the globe with the darkness of northern Canada, Alaska, much of Africa, central South America and Australia.

Several interesting details can be picked out, such as the spider-web

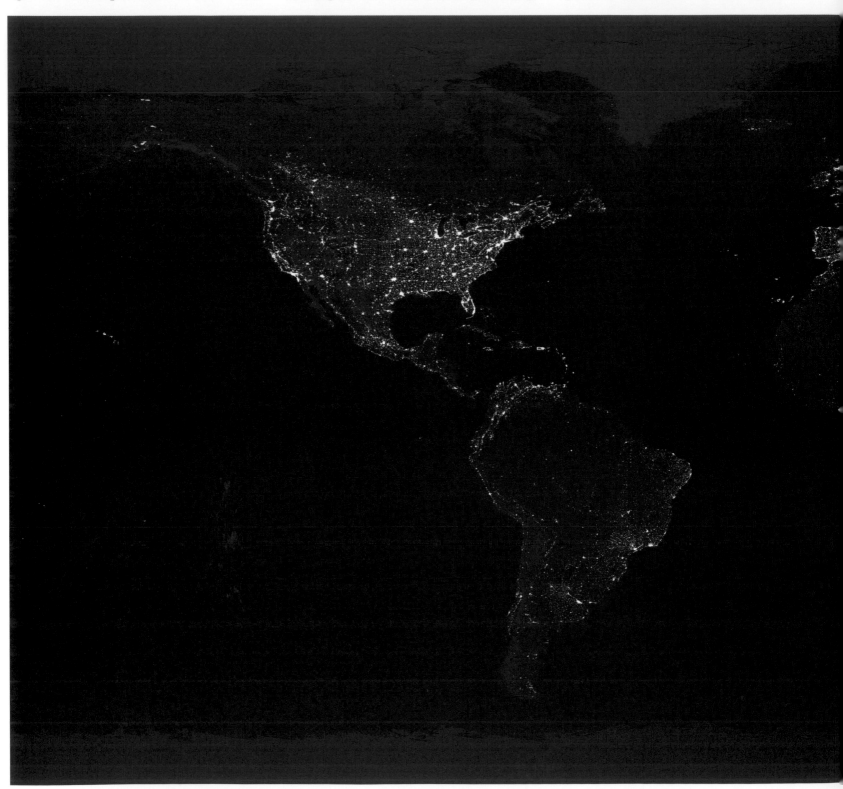

pattern of roads around Moscow, a chain of lights along the trans-Siberian railway extending eastwards from Moscow through Central Asia to Vladivostok, and in North Africa the Nile Valley from the Aswan Dam to the Mediterranean. Coastlines, such as those of California, Florida and the Mediterranean, are outlined by lights.

The United States interstate highway system appears as a lattice connecting the brighter dots of cities.

Various island groups stand out as bright points, such as Hawaii in the Pacific Ocean, the West Indies in the Caribbean Sea, the Canary Islands off the north-western coast of Africa, with the Azores farther out into the Atlantic

Ocean, and Réunion and Mauritius in the Indian Ocean to the east of Madagascar. Note how the lights of northern India delineate the arc of the Himalaya mountain range, and the abrupt border between energy-rich South Korea and the darker North Korea. Unpopulated Antarctica lies along the bottom of the image.

THE MOON

THE MOON is the Earth's companion in space, lying roughly 380,000 kilometres (240,000 miles) away, a distance that would take two or three days to travel in a spacecraft.

It is a ball of rock about one-quarter the size of our planet, with no air, water or life. It is the only other body in space on which human beings have ever set foot. American astronauts walked on the Moon during the Apollo space missions, from 1969 to 1972.

The Moon moves around the Earth, so it rises and sets at noticeably different times each night. As it orbits the

▲ *Three photographs of the Moon,* *taken at crescent phase, first quarter (half* *Moon), and full Moon. Some features* *change in appearance as the phase*

Earth, the Moon seems to change in shape – sometimes it is a crescent (curved), other times it is a half circle, and other times it is a full circle. These changes are known as the Moon's *phases*, and the diagram opposite explains how they occur. A complete cycle of phases lasts 29 days and is the origin of our month.

Even a quick glance at the Moon shows that it has dark markings which

changes. For example, the bright rays *surrounding a crater called Tycho stand out* *clearly at full Moon, but are scarcely* *noticeable only a few days before.*

form a pattern like a face, popularly known as 'the man in the Moon'. Every time we look at the Moon we see the same markings, which means that the Moon keeps the same side turned towards us. There is a very good reason for this. The Earth's pull of gravity has 'locked' the Moon so that it turns on its own axis in the same time as it takes to orbit the Earth.

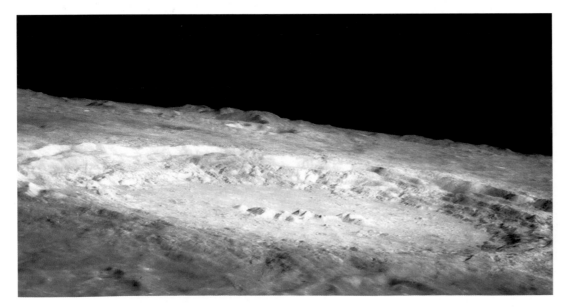

MOON DATA

DIAMETER:	3475 km
DISTANCE FROM EARTH:	384,400 km
TIME TO ORBIT EARTH:	27.32 days
TIME TO SPIN ON AXIS:	27.32 days
MASS:	0.0123 × Earth
VOLUME:	0.02 × Earth
AVERAGE DENSITY:	3.3 × water

◀ *One of the most prominent lunar* *craters is called Copernicus. This* *photograph of it was taken from the* *Apollo 12 spacecraft. Copernicus is* *93 kilometres (58 miles) across.*

Where did the Moon come from?

Astronomers are still not sure how the Moon was born. One old theory said it was a piece of the Earth that broke off long ago, when our planet was hot and spinning quickly. Another idea was that it was once a separate body that was captured by the Earth's gravity when it passed too close. In a third theory, the Moon supposedly grew from material left over from the birth of our planet. But there are problems with all three theories. A more recent theory says that the Moon originated in a huge collision between the Earth and another body. The other body was destroyed in the impact, but bits from it and the Earth were blasted into space. They created a ring around the Earth, and the debris gathered together to form the Moon.

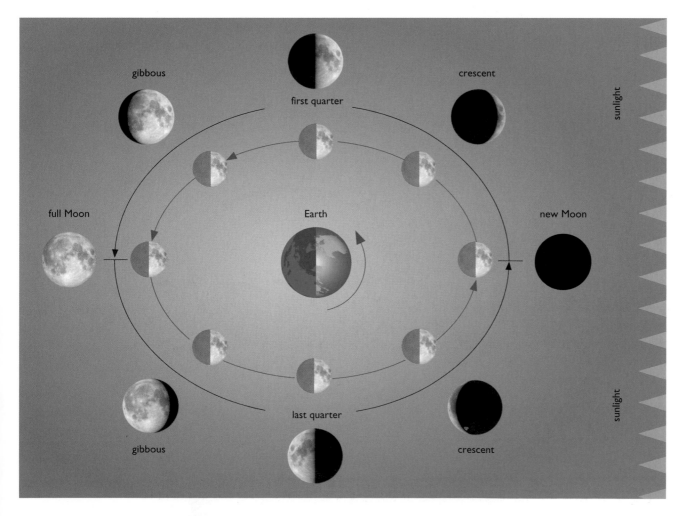

◀ **As the Moon** orbits the Earth, we see different amounts of its sunlit side. When the Moon lies between the Earth and the Sun we cannot see it at all; this is known as new Moon. Then it becomes a young crescent and appears low in the western sky after sunset. A few days later it becomes half-illuminated, when it is known as first quarter. The phase between half and full Moon is known as gibbous. After full Moon there are the same phases but in reverse order, ending with a crescent Moon rising in the morning sky shortly before the Sun.

THE MOON'S FEATURES

A simple pair of binoculars will show an amazing amount of detail on the Moon. There are dark, smooth lowlands and bright, mountainous areas dotted with craters of all sizes. The dark lowlands are called 'seas', although there is no liquid water on the Moon, nor has there ever been. The seas have fanciful names such as Mare Nubium (Sea of Clouds), Oceanus Procellarum (Ocean of Storms) and Mare Tranquillitatis (Sea of Tranquillity).

The craters were formed by meteorites and comets hitting the Moon long ago. The largest craters are over 100 kilometres (60 miles) across, large enough to swallow a city. They are named after scientists and other famous people. Asteroids also hit the Moon, digging out huge basins. These basins were later flooded by volcanic lava from inside the Moon, forming the seas.

The Moon's surface is incredibly ancient. Rocks from the lunar lowlands, brought back by Apollo astronauts, are

The far side

The Moon always keeps one face turned towards us, so no one had ever seen the far side of the Moon until space probes flew around it. They showed that most of the Moon's far side is covered with heavily cratered highlands, with few of the dark seas that are common on the Earth-facing side. The reason for this is that the Moon's crust is thicker on the far side, so that volcanic lava could not easily flow out onto the surface there.

▶ *Two photographs of the Moon, at first and last quarter, with some of the main features labelled. Capital letters are used for the names of lowland plains. Crater names start just to the right of each crater itself. To match these pictures with the view through a telescope, turn the book upside-down. Binoculars will show the Moon the 'right' way up, as it appears here.*

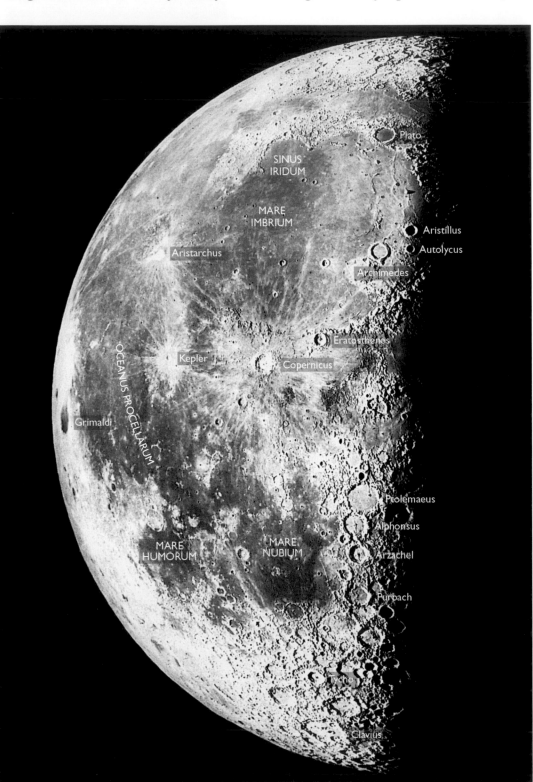

over 3000 million years old. The oldest rocks, from the Moon's highlands, are 4500 million years old, and so date back to the birth of the Moon.

The Moon has changed little since the seas were formed, apart from a few places where meteorites have formed new craters. You can easily spot the youngest craters, because they have long white rays stretching away from them. The rays are particularly bright at full Moon, and consist of rock thrown out by the impact that made the crater. Rays from one bright crater, Tycho, stretch over most of the Moon's near side. Tycho is about 100 million years old, one of the youngest of the large craters.

Man on the Moon

▲ **Apollo 17 astronaut Eugene Cernan** stands on the Moon in December 1972. At right is part of the electric car in which the astronauts explored the Moon's surface.

Neil Armstrong and Edwin Aldrin were the first humans to land on the Moon. They touched down on the Sea of Tranquillity on July 20, 1969, during the Apollo 11 mission. As Armstrong stepped onto the Moon, he said: "That's one small step for a man, one giant leap for mankind." Armstrong and Aldrin walked on the Moon for two hours, collecting 20 kilograms (48 lb) of rocks. Later Apollo missions took an electric Moon car which astronauts drove over the surface. In all, twelve Apollo astronauts walked on the Moon. The last mission, Apollo 17, was in December 1972.

▲ **Neil Armstrong,** the first human to set foot on the Moon, is pictured on this US stamp issued in 1969.

ECLIPSES AND TIDES

THE EARTH and Moon each cast a shadow into space, and an eclipse happens when one of them goes into the other's shadow. An eclipse of the Sun is when the Moon moves in front of the Sun, and its shadow falls on the Earth. An eclipse of the Moon is when the Earth's shadow falls on the Moon. There are at least two eclipses of the Sun every year and usually one or two of the Moon, but they cannot all be seen from one place on Earth.

Most spectacular are *total eclipses* of the Sun, when the Moon completely blots out the Sun's bright face and turns day into night for several minutes.

◀ *The Sun's beautiful corona,* a halo of gas, seen from Zambia during a total eclipse on 21 June, 2001.

▼ *How eclipses happen.* When the Moon's shadow falls on the Earth (below left), the Sun is eclipsed. The dark, inner part of the shadow is called the umbra. Where the path of the umbra passes across the Earth, people see a total eclipse. In the lighter, outer part of the shadow, the penumbra, the eclipse is partial. When the Earth's shadow falls on the Moon (below right), the Moon is eclipsed.

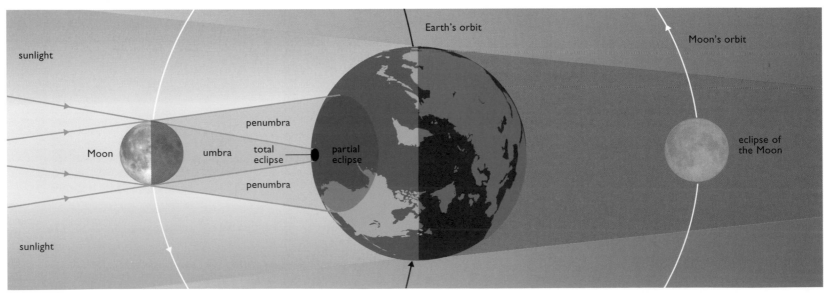

▲ *An eclipse of the Moon* in April 1996.

During a total solar eclipse, the faint halo of gas around the Sun, its corona, comes into view. Astronomers often travel the world to see a total eclipse of the Sun. A *partial eclipse*, in which the Sun is only partly covered by the Moon, is seen over a much wider area on Earth than the total eclipse.

Total solar eclipses are the result of a remarkable coincidence: the Moon and Sun appear almost exactly the same size in the sky. If the Moon were smaller, or farther away, it would not cover all of the Sun. In fact, the Moon's distance from Earth changes slightly, because its orbit is not exactly circular. If a solar eclipse happens when the Moon is at its most distant from us, the eclipse is not total. Instead, a ring of sunlight is left around the Moon at mid-eclipse. This is known as an *annular eclipse*, from a Latin word meaning 'ring'.

Total eclipses of the Sun can last up to seven and a half minutes, but most are much shorter. Total eclipses of the Moon can last for over an hour, and can be seen from anywhere the Moon is above the horizon. However, the Moon does not disappear, even when it lies entirely within the Earth's shadow and is totally eclipsed. Usually, it turns a dark red. This is because some of the Sun's light is bent through the Earth's atmosphere and falls onto the Moon.

Tides

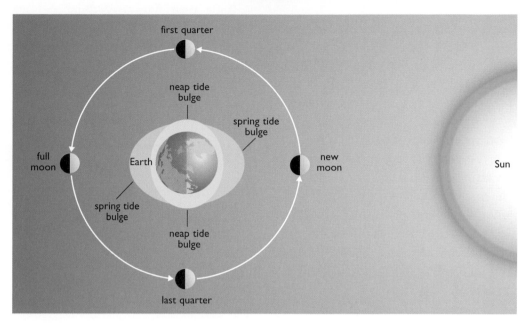

Tides are caused by the gravity of the Sun and Moon pulling on the oceans of the Earth, creating two bulges of water. The tidal pull of the Moon is greater than that of the Sun because it is much closer to us. The bulges in the oceans are highest when the Moon and Sun are pulling in line, at full Moon and new Moon. But when the Moon and Sun are at right angles to the Earth, at first and last quarter, the bulges are not so high. The oceans rise and fall as the Earth rotates under the bulges of water, so that most places have two high tides and two low tides each day.

▲ **The 250-kilometre (150-mile) long Bay of Fundy** in Canada has a bigger difference between tides than anywhere else on Earth – high tide there is nearly

15 metres (50 feet) higher than low tide. These photographs were taken at high and low tide at Hopewell Cape, on the New Brunswick side of the bay.

MERCURY

OF ALL the planets, closest to the Sun is Mercury, an airless ball of rock less than half the size of the Earth. It is difficult to see because it never strays far from the Sun. Even now, astronomers know little about it apart from some basic facts, which show that it is an odd world indeed.

For one thing, Mercury spins very slowly on its axis, once every 59 days. This is two-thirds of the time it takes to orbit the Sun. As a result, the Sun rises and sets very slowly as seen from Mercury. A 'day' on Mercury – say, from one noon to the next – lasts 176 Earth days. In that time, Mercury orbits the Sun twice and spins three times on its axis.

Perhaps the most puzzling fact about Mercury is its high density, which is second only to that of the Earth among all the planets. To explain this high density, Mercury must have an exceptionally large iron core, three-quarters the diameter of the planet itself. It is possible that Mercury was once much larger, and its rocky outer layers were then blasted off by large impacts shortly after it formed.

Few markings can be seen on Mercury, even through large telescopes. The first good look at its surface came from the US space probe Mariner 10 when it flew past Mercury in 1974. Mariner 10's cameras showed that Mercury looks a lot like our Moon. Mercury's surface is covered with craters up to 640 kilometres (400 miles) across. Like the craters on the Moon, they were formed when meteorites smashed into the planet's surface.

▶ *A mosaic of photographs from the space probe Mariner 10, whose path took it past Mercury twice in 1974 and again in 1975. On these three brief visits, Mariner 10 photographed half the planet's surface. Future space probes will finish the job.*

There may be surprises to come from Mercury. A US probe called Messenger will fly past Mercury twice, in 2007 and 2008, before going into orbit around it in 2009. Messenger will map the planet in detail, including the parts not yet seen, and study the composition of its surface rocks. Messenger is expected to be followed a few years later by a joint European–Japanese probe called BepiColombo.

In the daytime, Mercury's surface is seared by the Sun's rays, heating up to over 400°C, hot enough to melt tin and lead. At night, however, the temperature plunges to −170°C. Mercury is a hostile world. No one is likely to visit it for a long time to come, if ever.

MERCURY DATA

DISTANCE FROM SUN:	58 million km (average)
DIAMETER:	4880 km
TIME TO ORBIT SUN:	88 days
TIME TO SPIN ON AXIS:	59 days
MASS:	0.06 × Earth
VOLUME:	0.06 × Earth
AVERAGE DENSITY:	5.4 × water
TILT OF AXIS:	0°
NUMBER OF MOONS:	0

Mercury and the Mariner 10 space probe that first photographed its craters, shown on a US stamp.

▼ **The surface of Mercury** seems to have become wrinkled in places. This ridge, called Discovery Scarp, is about 350 kilometres (220 miles) long and passes through two older craters. Such wrinkles are thought to have formed when the planet cooled and shrank slightly.

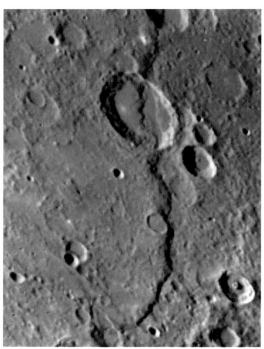

◀ **Craters abound** on the surface of Mercury. They look very much like the craters on the Moon and were formed in the same way, by meteorites crashing into the surface. The largest crater in the picture, containing a jagged mountain peak, is 63 kilometres (39 miles) across. It is named Nervo, after a Mexican poet.

Transits of Mercury

Sometimes the tiny disk of Mercury can be seen through a telescope crossing the face of the Sun. Such an event is called a *transit*. Transits of Mercury do not happen often: the next ones are in 2006, 2016 and 2019. This sequence of images of Mercury in transit in May 2003 was taken by the Sun-watching satellite called SOHO.

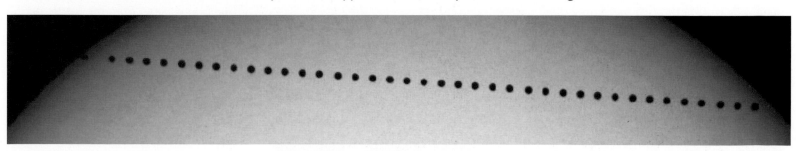

VENUS, THE HELL PLANET

VENUS is easy to spot when it shines brilliantly in the twilight as the morning or evening 'star' – far brighter than any true star. A small telescope shows that Venus is not a star at all, but a planet that goes through a cycle of phases as it orbits the Sun (see the diagram).

However, no telescope can show the surface of Venus because the planet is totally wrapped in clouds. It is sunlight reflected off these clouds that makes the planet so bright. Until space probes reached the planet astronomers could only guess what the surface was like.

Although Venus is almost the same size as the Earth, in many other ways the two planets are very different.

The first space probe to fly past Venus, Mariner 2 in 1962, found that the planet was scorchingly hot. Later probes landed on the planet's surface, and recorded oven-like temperatures of around 460°C, even at night.

The reason for these high temperatures is the atmosphere of Venus. It is almost entirely carbon dioxide – the gas that we breathe out. Carbon dioxide traps heat from the Sun very well, so underneath the clouds of Venus it has got hotter and hotter. This is an extreme example of what is called the *greenhouse effect*. Scientists are worried that a similar greenhouse effect will heat up the Earth if we let too much carbon dioxide from burning fuels get into our atmosphere.

As well as being baking hot and unbreathable, the atmosphere of Venus bears down on the planet's surface with a crushing force 90 times greater than the Earth's atmospheric pressure. No wonder the first Russian probes that parachuted down to its surface soon stopped working, although they did manage to send some pictures and other readings.

Adding to the Hellish nature of Venus is the composition of the clouds themselves. On Earth, clouds are made of water vapour, but there is no water on Venus. Its clouds consist of droplets of sulphuric acid, the same type of acid that is in a car battery. Who would ever want to go to Venus?

In 2006 a European Space Agency probe called Venus Express is planned to go into orbit around the planet to study its clouds and atmosphere.

▲ **An artist's impression** of a Russian Venera probe on Venus. These probes were heavily reinforced to withstand the immense pressures at the surface. Huge flashes of lightning may crackle through the murky air.

▼ **The rocky surface of Venus** as seen by Venera 13, showing part of the probe itself in the foreground. The strange orange light is produced by the dense clouds of sulphuric acid that envelop the planet.

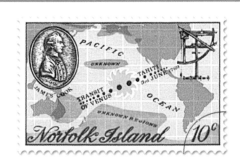

Venus occasionally crosses the face of the Sun as seen from the Earth, an event known as a transit. Transits of Venus are rare, and were once regarded as so scientifically important that Captain James Cook was sent to the Pacific Ocean in 1769 to observe one, an event commemorated on this stamp from Norfolk Island.

▶ **On its way to Mercury,** the US space probe Mariner 10 passed Venus and took this photograph of its yellowish-coloured clouds, which completely surround the planet and obscure its surface from view. The tops of the clouds lie 65 kilometres (40 miles) above the planet's surface. The clouds spiral from the equator to the pole and are almost featureless.

VENUS DATA

Distance from Sun:	108 million km
Diameter:	12,100 km
Time to orbit Sun:	225 days
Time to spin on axis:	243 days
Mass:	0.82 × Earth
Volume:	0.86 × Earth
Average density:	5.24 × water
Tilt of axis:	177°
Number of moons:	0

▼ **As Venus orbits the Sun,** it goes through phases similar to those of the Moon. Venus is at its brightest when it is a crescent. At its closest, Venus lies 40 million kilometres (25 million miles) from the Earth, closer than any other planet – although then it is between us and the Sun and cannot be seen.

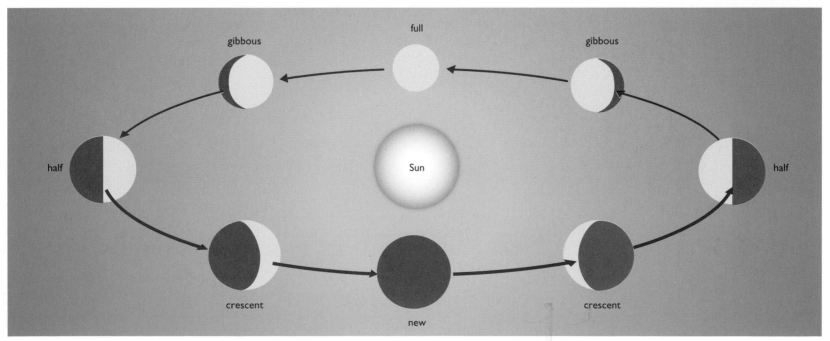

THE SURFACE OF VENUS

Beneath its clouds, Venus is a world with continents, rolling plains, canyons, volcanic mountains and meteorite craters. These features have been revealed by using radar to 'see' through the clouds, from space probes and from radio telescopes on Earth. The most detailed survey to date was made by the US space probe Magellan which went into orbit around Venus in 1990.

The highest point on Venus is a mountain range in the northern hemisphere, Maxwell Montes, named after a Scottish scientist, James Clerk Maxwell. Its summit towers 11 kilometres (7 miles) above the average surface level of Venus. (Because there is no water on Venus there is no such thing as 'sea level'.)

Maxwell Montes is part of a continent called Ishtar, the size of Australia. The largest continent on Venus, half the size of Africa, is Aphrodite, on the planet's equator. It includes the second-highest peak on Venus, Maat Mons, 8.5 kilometres (5 miles) high, seen in the picture below. Maat Mons is believed to be an active volcano, and it is likely that other mountains on Venus were also formed by volcanic eruptions. The Russian Venera probes that landed on Venus found that its surface rocks were similar to volcanic lava on Earth.

As well as volcanoes there are craters where large meteorites hit the planet. Even Venus's dense atmosphere is no protection against the largest meteorites.

Nearly all the features on Venus are named after women, real or mythical. For example, Ishtar and Aphrodite (after whom the main continents are named) were both goddesses, but many of the craters are named after women scientists and artists.

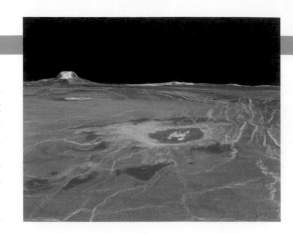

▲ *Part of Venus* known as Eistla Regio. To the right of centre is a crater called Cunitz, 48 kilometres (30 miles) wide. In the distance is Gula Mons, a volcano.

▼ *Gula Mons* from closer up. This volcano is 3 kilometres (2 miles) high, and it is surrounded by lava flows that stretch for hundreds of kilometres.

▼ *Maat Mons,* a volcano on Venus's equator that might still be active. The pictures on these pages were made by computer-processing radar maps from the Magellan probe to create three-dimensional views. The colour has been added to make them look more realistic. The height of the mountains has been 'stretched' so they look much steeper than they really are.

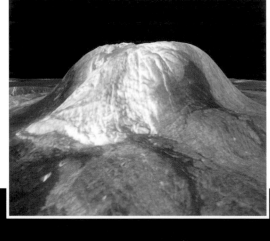

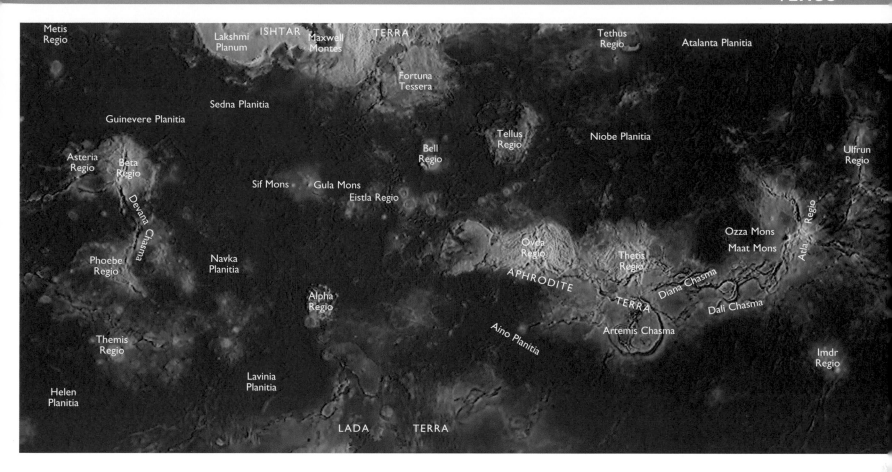

Metis Regio
Lakshmi Planum
ISHTAR
Maxwell Montes
TERRA
Tethus Regio
Atalanta Planitia
Fortuna Tessera
Sedna Planitia
Guinevere Planitia
Tellus Regio
Niobe Planitia
Ulfrun Regio
Asteria Regio
Beta Regio
Bell Regio
Sif Mons
Gula Mons
Eistla Regio
Ozza Mons
Maat Mons
Devana Chasma
Ovda Regio
Thetis Regio
Atla Regio
Phoebe Regio
Navka Planitia
APHRODITE
Diana Chasma
Dali Chasma
Alpha Regio
TERRA
Themis Regio
Aino Planitia
Artemis Chasma
Imdr Regio
Helen Planitia
Lavinia Planitia
LADA   TERRA

▲ **Map of Venus,** *coloured like maps of the Earth to show the height of the ground. Blue areas are lowest and red the highest, with green and yellow in between.*

The lowland plains are called planitiae. *Other terms used for features on the surface are* mons *(mountain),* regio *(region) and* chasma *(canyon).*

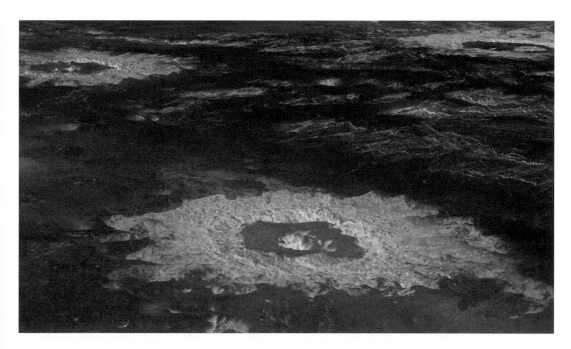

▲ **Three large craters** *on Venus caused by meteorite strikes. In the foreground is Howe (37 kilometres/23 miles wide). At top left is Danilova (48 kilometres/30 miles)* *and at top right is Aglaonice (64 kilometres/ 39 miles). They are surrounded by light-coloured fringes of rock ejected by the meteorite impact that formed them.*

The strange spin of Venus

Venus spins very slowly on its axis, once every 243 days. This is even longer than the time it takes to orbit the Sun, 225 days. Venus is the only planet that takes longer to spin than to orbit the Sun. Another odd fact is that it spins from east to west, which is the opposite direction to the spin of the Earth and other planets. No one knows why the spin of Venus should be so unusual. It is thought that perhaps another body hit it long ago, reversing its spin. The clouds of Venus move around the planet in the same back-to-front direction as the planet spins, that is, from east to west, but they do so much more quickly, every four days, blown by howling winds of 360 kilometres (220 miles) per hour or faster.

MARS, THE RED PLANET

MARS has long been thought of as the most likely planet on which we would find other life. Although it is only half the size of Earth, in some other ways it seems like our home planet.

The day on Mars is only just over half an hour longer than ours, and it has an atmosphere with clouds. There are polar caps that melt in summer and spread in winter, and deserts too.

Most interesting of all are dark markings that change slightly in size and shape each year. These were once thought to be areas where plants were growing. Even more sensationally, a century ago some astronomers thought they could see 'canals' on its surface, which they supposed were dug by Martian beings to bring water from the poles to the deserts.

Space probes have shown us many interesting things on Mars, but so far there has been no sign of life. Mars has turned out to be more hostile than it appeared. For a start, it is icy cold – even on a summer's day, the air temperature never rises above freezing point. What's more, the air on Mars is far too thin to breathe, and so much ultraviolet radiation from the Sun reaches the surface that it would kill anything living.

Water cannot exist on the surface today, because the temperature is too cold and the atmospheric pressure too low. The water on Mars is now frozen away beneath the surface and in the polar caps. But there are signs that liquid water ran over the surface in the past. Space probes that have landed on the surface have found evidence

▼ **The rusty red surface of Mars,** *showing a crater about 200 metres (650 feet) wide, photographed by NASA's Spirit rover. Many of the rocks scattered around on the surface were probably thrown out by the meteorite impact that caused the crater. A range of hills is visible on the far horizon.*

Exploring the surface of Mars

In 2004 two American Mars rovers called Spirit and Opportunity touched down on opposite sides of the red planet. These six-wheeled explorers were about the size of a supermarket trolley. Each carried cameras to photograph the rocky red surface of the planet as they drove around and instruments to analyse soil and rocks. Their studies confirmed that water had flowed over the surface at both sites in the past, an important finding for the possible existence of life. In 1976 two earlier American landers called Viking touched down to search for signs of life, but they found none. If there was once water on Mars then life may have arisen in the past, but present-day conditions are so harsh that life could now exist only beneath the surface. Future probes will bring samples of Martian rocks back to Earth for scientists to study. One day, humans will travel to Mars to explore its red deserts for themselves.

▼ **Mars** as seen through the Hubble Space Telescope in 2003, when the planet was at its closest to Earth for 60,000 years. The red deserts and dark markings can clearly be seen. The dark 'tongue' above right of centre is a highland called Syrtis Major. It was once thought to be covered with plant life, but is now known to be dark rock. To the south of it is the lowland basin Hellas. At the bottom is the south polar cap, tilted towards the Sun as summer comes to the southern hemisphere.

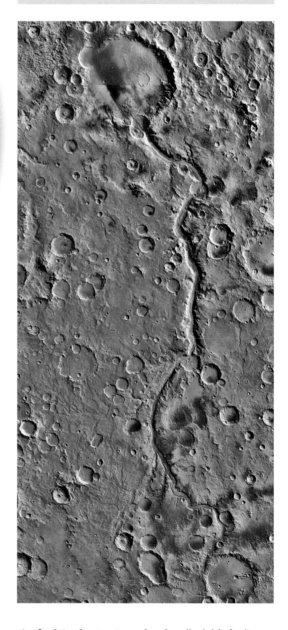

▲ **A dried-up river bed** called Ma'adim Vallis runs northwards into the crater Gusev, at the top of this picture. NASA's Spirit rover landed in Gusev in 2004 to look for signs of past water on Mars. Gusev is thought to have once been filled with a lake.

that water once flowed there, and there are markings that look like dried-up river beds. Perhaps Mars was warmer in the past, or perhaps eruptions of volcanoes and impacts of giant meteorites released water from beneath the crust.

The river beds photographed by space probes are not the 'canals'. Those seem to have been tricks of the eye, an optical illusion that fooled astronomers as they peered through their telescopes. The dark areas, once thought to be plants, are simply areas of darker rock and dust. They change in shape from year to year because the dust is blown around by winds.

This American stamp shows one of the two Viking landers which reached Mars in 1976. Each Viking probe came in two halves, one of which landed on the surface while the other remained in orbit. The lander used a long arm to scoop up soil samples.

29

THE VOLCANOES AND CANYONS OF MARS

Tourists who visit Mars in the future will want to see two things: its huge volcano, Olympus Mons, and a vast canyon system called the Mariner Valleys. Olympus Mons is larger than any volcano on Earth. It is shaped like a dome, 650 kilometres (400 miles) wide at its base and about 21 kilometres (13 miles) high, which would dwarf Mount Everest. At its summit is a crater 80 kilometres (50 miles) wide, big enough to swallow several cities. Near Olympus Mons is a row of three smaller (but still very large) volcanoes in an area called the Tharsis Ridge.

To the east of the Tharsis Ridge lie the Mariner Valleys (or Valles Marineris), named after the Mariner 9 spacecraft which first photographed them in 1971. The whole valley complex is 4000 kilometres (2500 miles) long, enough to stretch across the United States. In the middle it is as much as 10 kilometres (6 miles) deep and 600 kilometres (375 miles) wide.

Although called a 'canyon', it is not like the Grand Canyon in the United States, which was carved out by a river and is much smaller. Instead, Valles Marineris is more like the Rift Valley of East Africa. It was formed by cracking in the crust of Mars. Landslides, winds and running water have since helped to enlarge the canyons.

Other parts of Mars look like the Moon. Most of the planet's southern hemisphere, for example, is highlands

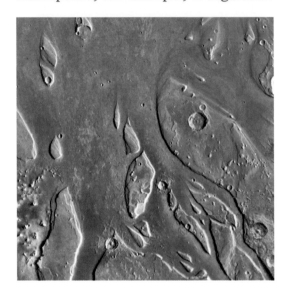

with craters made by meteorites, not volcanoes. One large feature in the southern hemisphere is a lowland plain like one of the lunar maria or 'seas'. Called Hellas, it is about 2000 kilometres (1250 miles) wide and 8 kilometres (5 miles) deep. It is thought to have been dug out by a meteorite that hit Mars 3500 million years ago. Other large impact basins are Argyre, also in the southern hemisphere, and Isidis, near the Martian equator.

◀ **Ancient floods** washed over this area on Mars, called Tiu Vallis, eroding the surface and creating these islands. The water is thought to have burst out from beneath the surface of Mars. In this area it flowed from south to north, spreading out and probably evaporating as it did so.

▼ **A map of Mars,** colour-coded to show different heights. Blue and green areas are the lowest; red, brown and white are the highest. Major mountains, plains and craters are labelled. This map was made by NASA's Mars Global Surveyor spacecraft.

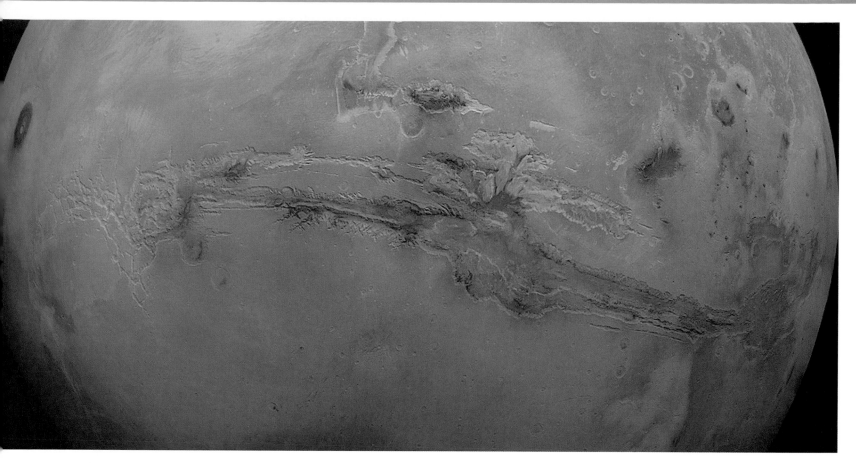

▲ **The system of Martian canyons** called Valles Marineris, partly filled with dark dust, crosses this picture. It starts in a cracked region known as Noctis Labyrinthus and opens out into Chryse Planitia in the east. The two dark spots at far left are the volcanoes Pavonis Mons and Arsia Mons.

▼◄ **Olympus Mons,** below, the biggest volcano in the Solar System, viewed at an angle. The mountain and its clouds can be seen through a telescope from Earth. Left, a close-up of the crater at its summit.

Moons of Mars

Mars has two moons, Phobos and Deimos. They are both small and oddly shaped, like lumpy potatoes. Phobos, below left, is only 27 kilometres (17 miles) at its widest, and Deimos is 15 kilometres (9 miles) across. Both moons have been cratered by meteorites. Phobos and Deimos are thought to be ex-asteroids that were captured into orbit around Mars.

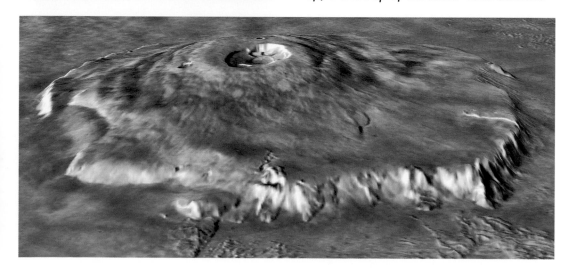

JUPITER, THE GIANT PLANET

BEYOND MARS and the asteroid belt, the planets change from being small and rocky to being large and made of gas and liquid. Largest of all is Jupiter, eleven times wider than the Earth and over twice as massive as all the other planets put together. It never comes closer to us than about 600 million kilometres (370 million miles), but because of its large size it still shines more brightly than any star in the night sky.

Jupiter is made mostly of hydrogen and helium. On the Earth, hydrogen and helium are gases. But under the tremendous pressures inside a planet as big as Jupiter they are squeezed into a liquid. So Jupiter is mostly a ball of liquid hydrogen and helium, covered with a layer of clouds. There is no solid surface for a spaceship to land on.

Jupiter's clouds are drawn out into bands by the planet's fast spin – its 'day' lasts less than 10 hours. Jupiter bulges at the equator because it spins so quickly. Various chemicals turn the clouds white, yellow, brown and red in colour.

The weather on Jupiter is stormy, and the clouds change in appearance as they swirl around the planet. Only one feature, a big storm cloud called the Great Red Spot, seems to be there all the time. In 1979 two space probes called Voyager flew past the planet and photographed the clouds in detail, as did the Cassini probe on its way to Saturn in 2000. These probes also saw flashes of lightning on the night side of Jupiter, caused by thunderstorms.

In 1995 a space probe called Galileo went into orbit around Jupiter. It released a smaller probe that para-chuted down through the clouds, telling us more about the winds and temperatures there. The probe was eventually crushed when the pressure became too great for it to withstand.

JUPITER DATA	
DISTANCE FROM SUN:	778 million km
DIAMETER:	143,000 km (at the equator)
TIME TO ORBIT SUN:	11.9 years
TIME TO SPIN ON AXIS:	9 hr 50 min (at the equator)
MASS:	318 × Earth
VOLUME:	1321 × Earth
AVERAGE DENSITY:	1.3 × water
TILT OF AXIS:	3.1°
NUMBER OF MOONS:	60+

The first probe to reach Jupiter was Pioneer 10, which flew past the planet in 1973, as commemorated on this US stamp. Pioneer 10 was followed by Pioneer 11, which also became the first probe to reach Saturn.

▲ **Jupiter** as photographed by the Cassini space probe in December 2000 when it flew past the giant planet on its way to Saturn. Colourful bands of clouds cross the face of Jupiter. At lower right is the Great Red Spot, a storm cloud larger than the Earth. The black spot at left is the shadow of one of Jupiter's moons, Europa.

The comet that crashed into Jupiter

In July 1994 more than 20 pieces from a broken-up comet called Shoemaker–Levy 9 plunged into the atmosphere of Jupiter, leaving a series of dusty markings in the planet's clouds. Some of the dark marks can be seen in this photograph taken by the Hubble Space Telescope a few days after the collisions. The largest marking, seen in close-up in the smaller picture, looked like an eye and was as large as the Earth. Over a period of more than a year, the dust clouds spread out and eventually faded away.

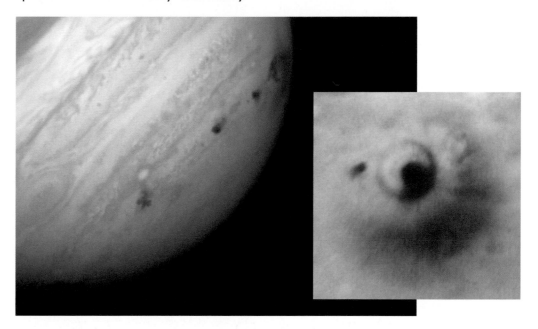

▲ *In this close-up of Jupiter's clouds from the Cassini space probe, the colours have been altered to bring out details. Red regions are low clouds, while bright blue regions are high haze. The darkest blue areas are the deepest clouds of all. White spots are storms high in the atmosphere. Winds blowing at 450 kilometres (275 miles) per hour create complicated and beautiful patterns in the clouds.*

Jupiter's Great Red Spot

In Jupiter's southern hemisphere is a large cloud shaped like an eye. It is called the Great Red Spot, and was first seen when astronomers turned their telescopes on the planet in the 17th century. The Great Red Spot is about 25,000 kilometres (15,000 miles) long and 12,000 kilometres (7500 miles) wide, although it changes somewhat in size and shape with time. It is big enough to swallow several Earths. The spot's red colour is thought to come from phosphorus, the same substance as in the heads of red matches. It seems to be a spinning storm cloud, caused by gas rising from Jupiter's warm interior.

THE MOONS OF JUPITER

Jupiter has over 60 known moons, more than any other planet. The four biggest and brightest moons were discovered by the Italian scientist Galileo Galilei in 1610. An ordinary pair of binoculars shows them as tiny points of light, moving around the planet from night to night.

In order of distance from the planet they are called Io, Europa, Ganymede and Callisto. Of the four, Io is the most interesting because it has active volcanoes which have been photographed erupting by the Voyager and Galileo space probes. They do not erupt normal lava like volcanoes on Earth but instead spray out sulphur and sulphur dioxide. The sulphur gives the surface a peculiar orange colour. Io is thought to be kept hot by Jupiter's strong gravity, which 'squeezes' the moon, releasing heat.

By contrast, the next moon, Europa, is covered with white ice. Most of its surface is smooth, but in places it is cracked like an eggshell. Ganymede is

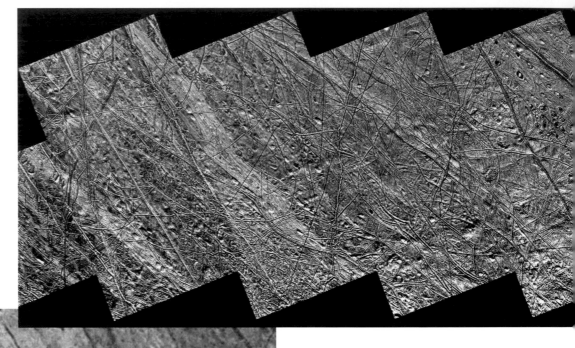

▶ *Europa has a bright, icy surface criss-crossed by a network of lines, some stretching for thousands of kilometres. These may be places where water once flowed up through cracks in the ice and then froze. The bull's-eye feature at right is an impact crater in the ice, seen by the Galileo space probe.*

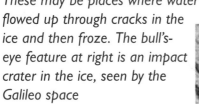

the largest moon in the Solar System, larger than the planet Mercury, while Callisto is not much smaller than Mercury. Both Ganymede and Callisto are peppered with craters caused by meteorites. As well as craters, Ganymede has strange grooves on its surface, probably due to movements in the crust. The surfaces of these two moons are not rocky, like our own Moon, but consist of dirty ice.

All the other moons of Jupiter are smaller than the big four. The smallest of Jupiter's moons are only about 3 kilometres (2 miles) across, and more are being discovered all the time.

◀ **Io, Jupiter's volcanic moon,** *as seen by NASA's Galileo space probe. The large reddish-orange ring in the image at far left consists of sulphur ejected from a volcanic vent named Pele, after a Hawaiian volcano goddess. In the close-up of Io's multi-coloured surface, red and orange markings are thought to be compounds of sulphur while white patches are sulphur dioxide. Of all the discoveries made during our exploration of the Solar System, the volcanoes of Io were among the most unexpected.*

JUPITER'S MAIN MOONS DATA

Io

DIAMETER:	3643 km
DISTANCE FROM JUPITER:	422,000 km
TIME TO ORBIT JUPITER:	1.77 days

Europa

Diameter:	3124 km
Distance from Jupiter:	671,000 km
Time to orbit Jupiter:	3.55 days

Ganymede

DIAMETER:	5265 km
DISTANCE FROM JUPITER:	1.07 million km
TIME TO ORBIT JUPITER:	7.16 days

Callisto

DIAMETER:	4819 km
DISTANCE FROM JUPITER:	1.88 million km
TIME TO ORBIT JUPITER:	16.69 days

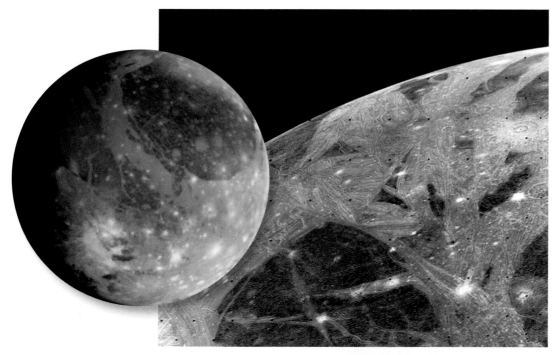

▲ **Faint rings of dust** *encircle Jupiter's equator. The densest part of the ring, which lies about 50,000 kilometres (30,000 miles) above the planet's cloud tops, is seen nearly edge-on in this view from Voyager 2.*

▲ **Ganymede, Jupiter's largest moon,** also has an icy surface but with some dark areas and bright spots due to young impact craters. The largest dark area is named Galileo, after the astronomer who discovered the moons of Jupiter. Strange ridges and grooves are found on the surface of this moon, as the close-up shows.

▶ **Callisto, the outermost of Jupiter's four largest moons,** has an ancient surface covered with craters of all sizes. The largest impact on this moon caused a scar named Valhalla, visible just above centre in the image at right. The bright central region of Valhalla is surrounded by a pattern of cracks, seen in more detail in the image on the far right.

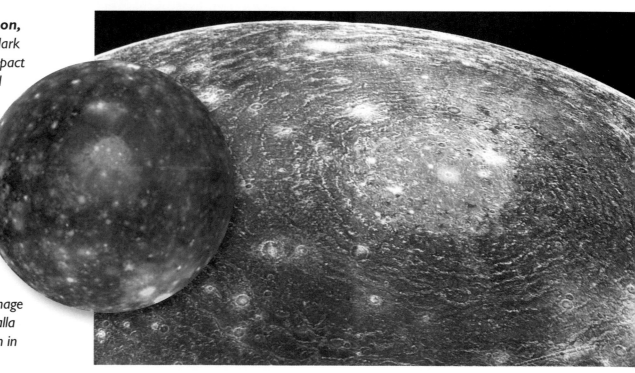

SATURN, THE RINGED PLANET

SATURN and its rings are one of the most beautiful sights in the night sky when seen through a telescope. In many ways Saturn is like a smaller version of Jupiter, although it does not have the same colourful bands of cloud in its atmosphere. There are cloud features, but they seem to be masked by a high-altitude layer of haze that gives the whole planet a smooth, yellowish look.

Every 30 years or so, a large white spot appears on Saturn. The last one, in 1990, was followed by several smaller outbreaks. These spots are actually bright clouds that form during summer in the planet's northern hemisphere. Summer comes only every 30 years on Saturn because that is how long the planet takes to orbit the Sun.

More than 30 moons have been discovered around Saturn, and there are probably other small ones as yet unseen. The largest of them, Titan, is the only moon in the Solar System with an atmosphere to speak of. Saturn's other moons are mostly chunks of ice

▲ **Saturn and its magnificent rings** *as seen through the Hubble Space Telescope. The Earth would fit three times over into*

and rock. One, called Mimas, has a huge crater on it. The meteorite that caused the crater must have almost broken Mimas apart. Another odd-looking moon, Iapetus, has one bright side, covered with ice, and one dark side, coated with dust or perhaps some other material. No one knows for certain why the two halves of Iapetus are so different.

the gap between the inner ring and the planet's surface. Note the dark gap in the rings known as the Cassini Division.

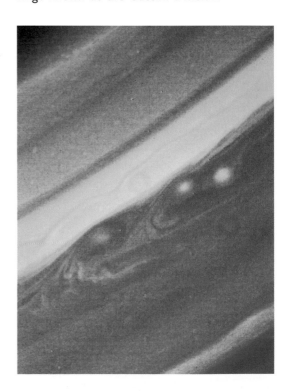

▲ **Saturn's atmosphere** *is not as stormy as that of Jupiter, but it does show a similar pattern of cloud bands. Colour has been added to this photograph to bring out detail.*

SATURN DATA	
DISTANCE FROM SUN:	1427 million km
DIAMETER:	120,500 km (at the equator)
TIME TO ORBIT SUN:	29.4 years
TIME TO SPIN ON AXIS:	10 hr 14 min (at the equator)
MASS:	95 × Earth
VOLUME:	764 × Earth
AVERAGE DENSITY:	0.7 × water
TILT OF AXIS:	26.7°
NUMBER OF MOONS:	30+

Titan

▲ **Saturn's moon Mimas,** 390 kilometres (240 miles) wide, has a huge crater called Herschel, one-third its own width. The crater has a big central peak.

▲ **Dione,** 1120 kilometres (700 miles) wide, has a mixture of lightly and heavily cratered areas, surface cracks and wispy marks that may be debris from impact craters or frost.

Titan, Saturn's main moon, is the second-largest moon in the Solar System. Only Jupiter's biggest moon, Ganymede, is larger. But what makes Titan unique among moons is that it is the only one to have a thick atmosphere. This atmosphere is mostly nitrogen, the main gas in our atmosphere on the Earth, plus some methane. Titan has been called a 'deep-freeze' version of the Earth. Normally we cannot see the surface of Titan because of smoggy clouds, which give it an orange appearance as in this Voyager 1 image (above left). However, infrared wavelengths pass through the clouds, so by observing at these wavelengths with the Hubble Space Telescope astronomers have been able to make rough maps of

Titan. The bright area in the image shown above right is thought to be a continent similar in size to Australia. Titan is so cold, because it is so far from the Sun, that methane may fall as rain on the surface, perhaps building up pools of oily liquid. A space probe called Huygens was due to land on Titan in January 2005. This probe is part of the joint US–European space mission to Saturn named Cassini after an astronomer who studied the planet in the 17th century.

TITAN DATA	
DIAMETER:	5150 km
DISTANCE FROM SATURN:	1.22 million km
TIME TO ORBIT SATURN:	15.9 days

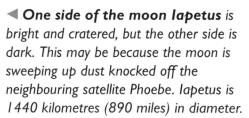

◀ **One side of the moon Iapetus** is bright and cratered, but the other side is dark. This may be because the moon is sweeping up dust knocked off the neighbouring satellite Phoebe. Iapetus is 1440 kilometres (890 miles) in diameter.

▶ **The most prominent features in Saturn's clouds** are large white spots that break out near the planet's equator from time to time. This one, photographed in 1994 by the Hubble Space Telescope, lasted for several months.

SATURN'S RINGS

Around Saturn's middle lies a set of bright rings. At first sight the rings look solid. But in fact they are made up of countless millions of frozen lumps that range in size from icebergs to snowballs. They all orbit Saturn like a swarm of tiny moons.

As seen from the Earth, the rings divide into three main bands, each of different brightness. The brightest part is in the middle, called the B ring. Outside it is the A ring, and between them is a gap called Cassini's Division, the width of the Atlantic Ocean. Closest to the planet is the faintest ring of the three, called the C ring or crepe ring.

The rings measure 270,000 kilometres (170,000 miles) from side to side, more than twice the width of the planet itself. Yet they are no more than a few hundred metres thick. In relation to their width, they are as thin as a sheet of paper the size of a football field. At

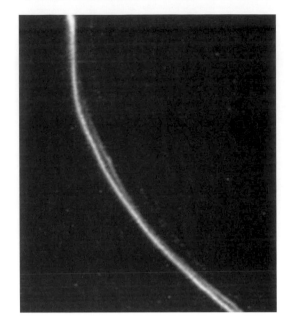

times the rings are tilted edge-on to us, when they almost disappear from view.

Our first detailed look at the rings was given by the two Voyager space probes, which flew past the planet in 1980 and 1981. In close-up, the smooth-looking rings broke up into

◄▲ *The strange F ring of Saturn* *is twisted, split and uneven (left). This odd appearance is caused by two tiny moons, called shepherd moons, which orbit either side of it and pull it out of shape. The two moons are seen in the photograph above, taken by the Cassini space probe in 2004.*

thousands of thin ringlets, like threads. In photographs like the ones on these pages, Saturn's system of rings looks like an enormous gramophone record. Even the Cassini Division contains some ringlets. Some other faint rings that cannot be seen from Earth were

▼ *Saturn's C ring* *reveals complex structure in this image from the Voyager 2 spacecraft, which has been computer-enhanced to bring out details. More than 60 bright and dark ringlets can be counted here. Material in the C ring appears the colour of dirty ice whereas the B ring, at top and left, appears golden yellow.*

▲ *Computer-processing brings out colour differences* *in Saturn's rings. The inner ring, the C ring, shows up blue, the B ring changes from orange to blue-green,* and the outer A ring appears blue-grey. The different colours may indicate differences in composition of the material that makes up the various parts of the rings.

Spokes

Photographs taken by the Voyager space probes showed strange dark patches that come and go on Saturn's rings. Scientists termed them 'spokes'. They are thought to be clouds of dust, possibly caused by the impact of meteorites on the rings.

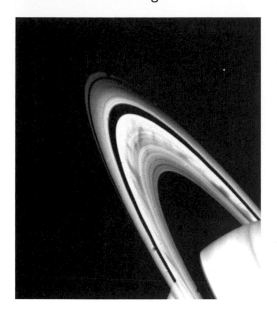

Cassini is a joint US–European space mission to Saturn. Cassini went into orbit around Saturn in July 2004 while a small lander, called Huygens, was due to descend to the surface of Saturn's largest moon, Titan, in January 2005.

discovered inside the C ring and beyond the A ring.

Most fascinating of these is the F ring, which looks twisted. The F ring is narrow, only a few hundred kilometres wide, and lies a few thousand kilometres beyond the outer edge of the A ring. Two small moons, Prometheus and Pandora, orbit either side of it. The gravity of these small moons pulls the ring particles out of their normal orbits, giving the ring its odd shape.

How were the rings of Saturn formed? Even now, scientists are not sure. They could be material left over from the birth of the planet itself. Or they could be the remains of a moon that strayed too close to the planet and broke up. Other theories are that the ring particles come from collisions between moons, or are the remains of comets that either crashed into moons or broke up after being captured. Perhaps more than one of these events gave rise to the rings we see today.

▲ *A crescent Saturn,* seen from the Voyager 1 probe after it passed the planet in 1980. The rings cast their narrow shadow on the planet's clouds, while at left the shadow of the planet falls across the rings. The planet can be seen through the thinnest parts of the rings where they cross in front of the sunlit globe at the bottom.

URANUS, THE TILTED PLANET

URANUS was the first planet to be discovered with a telescope. At its brightest it can just be seen with the naked eye, like a faint star, if you know where to look. But no one had ever noticed it before 1781, when William Herschel first spotted it through his telescope from his back garden in Bath, England. Uranus lies twice as far from the Sun as Saturn, so the discovery doubled the size of the known Solar System overnight.

Uranus is four times wider than the Earth and is covered in greenish clouds. The green colour is caused by methane gas in its atmosphere. However, only about 2% of the planet's atmosphere is methane – most of it consists of hydrogen and helium, the same composition as Jupiter and Saturn.

There are very few markings in the clouds of Uranus. Even the Voyager 2 space probe, which flew past the planet in 1986, found few cloud features of note. Underneath the clouds there is thought to be a deep ocean of water, methane and ammonia.

One remarkable fact about Uranus is that it is tilted on its side. As a result, the Sun can at times appear overhead at the poles. Uranus probably got its tilt long ago, when it was hit by another body. The collision literally knocked Uranus over so that its axis of rotation lies almost in the plane of its orbit.

▲ **Uranus is shrouded in greenish clouds,** *as seen here by the Voyager 2 space probe. When Voyager arrived, there was little sign of activity – there were few of the spots and storms seen on the other giant planets.*

The rings of Uranus

Uranus is encircled by a number of thin rings, too faint to see through telescopes on the Earth except at infrared wavelengths. They were first discovered in 1977, when Uranus moved in front of a star. The rings made the star's light flash on and off as they passed across it. Eleven rings are now known, including two discovered by Voyager 2. Unlike the bright rings of Saturn, they are as black as coal, which is why they are so difficult to see from Earth.

▲ **Uranus photographed by the Hubble Space Telescope,** *showing its rings, some moons and a chain of bright clouds north of its equator. The image was taken in the infrared and the colours are not real.*

URANUS DATA	
DISTANCE FROM SUN:	2870 million km
DIAMETER:	51,100 km (at the equator)
TIME TO ORBIT SUN:	84 years
TIME TO SPIN ON AXIS:	17 hr 14 min
MASS:	14.5 × Earth
VOLUME:	63 × Earth
AVERAGE DENSITY:	1.3 × water
TILT OF AXIS:	97.8°
NUMBER OF MOONS:	20+

▼ **The four largest moons of Uranus.** *From the left, and in order of distance from the planet, they are: Ariel (diameter 1160 kilometres/720 miles);* Umbriel (1170 kilometres/ 715 miles); Titania (1580 kilometres/980 miles); and Oberon (1520 kilometres/ 940 miles). All are icy, cratered worlds. Ariel has many cliffs and valleys. The dark surface of Umbriel has one bright spot, a 110-kilometre (70-mile) crater called Wunda. On Titania, there are valleys and fractures that cut through craters. Oberon has large impact craters surrounded by bright rays. These pictures were taken by Voyager 2.

Uranus has over 20 known moons, many of which were discovered by the Voyager 2 space probe. The most interesting of the moons is Miranda, pictured here. It has such a varied surface that scientists once thought it had been broken apart in the past and the parts had gathered themselves together again. However, it now seems that Miranda's odd surface features are actually the result of movements of ice. Uranus also has a number of faint, narrow rings around its equator.

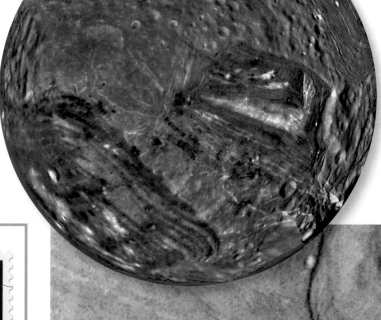

◄ **Remarkable Miranda –** *no other body has such a dramatic mixture of surface types. There are grooves, ridges and craters, as well as features not seen anywhere else, like the tick-shaped marking near the centre, nicknamed 'the Chevron'. At bottom right of the main picture, and shown in the close-up below, is a cliff that towers 20 kilometres (12 miles) above the moon's surface, over ten times deeper than the Grand Canyon. Miranda is 470 kilometres (290 miles) in diameter.*

URANUS VOYAGER 2 **29** USA

Our best views of Uranus came in 1986 when the US space probe Voyager 2 flew past the planet, photographing its clouds, rings and moons, as commemorated on this stamp.

NEPTUNE, THE BLUE GIANT

EARLY in the 19th century, astronomers noticed that Uranus was not keeping to its expected orbit. They guessed the reason was that the gravity of an unknown planet was pulling it off course.

Two men, John Couch Adams in England and Urbain Le Verrier in France, set out to calculate where that unknown planet might lie. Both men came up with similar answers. When a German astronomer, Johann Galle, looked near the predicted position in 1846, he found Neptune. It had never been noticed before because it was too distant and faint.

Neptune is four times the width of the Earth, almost as large as Uranus. Through a telescope Neptune appears blue-green. This colour is caused by methane gas in its atmosphere, as is the colour of Uranus.

Little was known about Neptune until the Voyager 2 space probe passed it in 1989. Neptune is so far away that Voyager 2's radio messages, travelling

▲ **Neptune's blue disk** seen by the American space probe Voyager 2. The atmosphere of Neptune is more active than that of Uranus. Visible in this photograph are dark spots and white clouds of methane ice crystals that look like the Earth's cirrus clouds.

at the speed of light, took over four hours to reach the Earth.

The most striking feature among Neptune's blue-green clouds was a dark spot the size of the Earth. This spot is thought to have been a storm cloud, similar to the Great Red Spot of Jupiter. Unlike the Great Red Spot, though, it was relatively short-lived and had vanished by 1994 when the Hubble Space Telescope took its first look at Neptune.

Like Uranus, Neptune turned out to have faint rings. Voyager discovered six new moons around Neptune to add to the two already known, Triton and Nereid. Other moons of Neptune have since been discovered from Earth, bringing the total to more than a dozen.

An imaginary view from the surface of Neptune's largest moon, Triton, is shown on this stamp from Ciskei, a former independent state within South Africa. The view is based on data from NASA's Voyager 2 space probe which reached Neptune in 1989 after a 12-year journey from the Earth.

NEPTUNE DATA	
DISTANCE FROM SUN:	4500 million km
DIAMETER:	49,500 km (at the equator)
TIME TO ORBIT SUN:	164.8 years
TIME TO SPIN ON AXIS:	16 hr 7 min
MASS:	17.2 × Earth
VOLUME:	58 × Earth
AVERAGE DENSITY:	1.6 × water
TILT OF AXIS:	28.3°
NUMBER OF MOONS:	12+

▼ **The Great Dark Spot** on Neptune looked like a darker version of Jupiter's Great Red Spot. Like Jupiter's spot, it was probably a spinning storm cloud, with gas rising from below. It was about 12,000 kilometres (7500 miles) long.

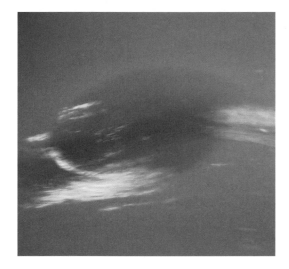

▲ **Neptune's second-biggest moon,** called Proteus, was discovered by Voyager 2. It is an irregularly shaped body, about 420 kilometres (260 miles) across, 50 kilometres or so bigger than Nereid. It takes just over a day to orbit Neptune.

▼ **Neptune's two brightest rings,** called Adams and Leverrier, are shown in this Voyager 2 image. Adams, the outer ring, has denser clumps of dust in it, termed ring arcs. The overexposed crescent of the planet itself is seen at bottom right.

Triton

Neptune's largest moon, Triton, is covered with pink and bluish ice, as shown in these images by Voyager 2. The ice consists of frozen nitrogen and methane at a temperature of −236°C, making it the coldest known place in the Solar System. Some of this ice evaporates to form a very thin atmosphere. Most astounding of all are the volcanoes of liquid nitrogen that erupt from pools beneath Triton's surface, spraying material nearly as high as Mount Everest.

Where this material falls back on to Triton it produces dark streaks, as seen in the smaller picture. Long ago, Triton probably orbited the Sun separately but was captured by Neptune's gravity when it strayed too close.

TRITON DATA	
DIAMETER:	2700 km
DISTANCE FROM NEPTUNE:	355,000 km
TIME TO ORBIT NEPTUNE:	5.9 days

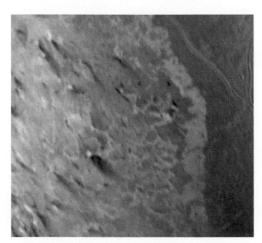

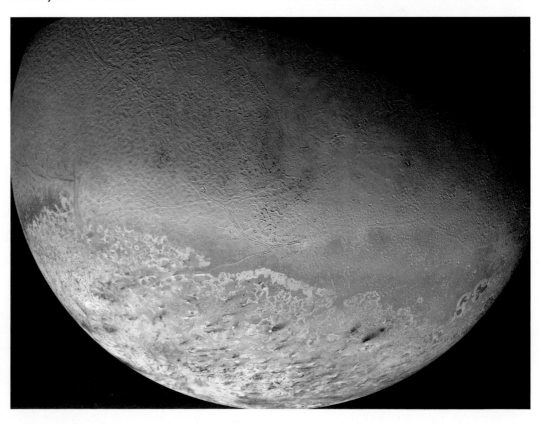

PLUTO, AT THE EDGE OF DARKNESS

PLUTO is the outermost planet, orbiting in the cold and dark far from the Sun. It was found in 1930 by an American astronomer, Clyde Tombaugh, during a careful search for undiscovered planets beyond Neptune. Astronomers had expected to find another large planet like Uranus or Neptune, but were surprised when Pluto turned out to be the smallest of all the planets, smaller even than our own Moon and Neptune's moon Triton.

Another peculiarity of Pluto is its orbit. At times, Pluto can come closer to the Sun than Neptune, as it did between the years 1979 and 1999.

Fortunately, there is no chance of a collision between the two planets. Their orbits are like two hoops, one tilted relative to the other so that they do not actually meet at any point.

We do not have any close-up photographs of Pluto because no space probe has been there yet. However, astronomers think that Pluto has ice on its surface and looks much like Triton. In fact, Triton may once have orbited the Sun at the edge of the Solar System, like Pluto. Triton could have been captured by Neptune's gravity to become a moon, while Pluto remained free.

In recent years, astronomers have discovered a swarm of small, icy bodies orbiting beyond Neptune. These are known as *trans-Neptunian objects,* and it seems that Pluto is simply the largest of them. NASA is planning to launch a mission called New Horizons in 2006, which will reach Pluto and Charon in 2016 and then fly on to examine other trans-Neptunian objects. It is unlikely that there are any large planets to be discovered beyond Pluto.

▼ *We can only guess what Pluto and its moon Charon might look like until a space probe gets there. A Pluto probe could be launched to arrive at the remote planet by 2016. This artist's impression shows Charon in the sky above Pluto, with the Sun just a bright spot in the distance.*

PLUTO DATA

DISTANCE FROM SUN:	4437 million km to 7376 million km
DIAMETER:	2390 km
TIME TO ORBIT SUN:	247.9 years
TIME TO SPIN ON AXIS:	6 days 9 hr
MASS:	0.002 × Earth
VOLUME:	0.007 × Earth
AVERAGE DENSITY:	1.8 × water
TILT OF AXIS:	122.5°
NUMBER OF MOONS:	1

Pluto is the only planet that has not yet been reached by a space probe.

Pluto's moon

Pluto has one moon, Charon, discovered in 1978. Charon is half the size of Pluto. This is larger in relation to the planet itself than any other moon (our own Moon, for example, is one-quarter the width of the Earth). Hence Pluto and Charon can be said to be a double planet. Charon orbits Pluto every 6.4 days, the same time the planet takes to spin on its own axis. As a result, the moon remains over one side of Pluto all the time and cannot be seen from the other side.

▲ *Pluto, left, and Charon, its moon,* seen through the Hubble Space Telescope. The two bodies are 19,600 kilometres (12,200 miles) apart, one-twentieth the distance between the Earth and our Moon.

▶ *Pluto,* seen through the Hubble Space Telescope. The bright and dark areas are thought to be caused by patches of frost on its surface. Close-up, Pluto probably looks like Neptune's largest moon, Triton.

◀ *Clyde Tombaugh* searched for a new planet by photographing a small part of the night sky, waiting a few days, and then photographing it again. A planet would move and therefore be in different places on the two pictures. Eventually he found what he was looking for on these photographs, which show part of the constellation Gemini. The arrows point to Pluto. Tombaugh carried on looking for several years, but found no more planets.

COMETS, GHOSTLY WANDERERS

AT THE edge of the Solar System, far beyond Neptune and Pluto, a huge swarm of comets orbits the Sun. The comet swarm is known as the *Oort Cloud*, after the Dutch astronomer Jan Oort, who suggested its existence. Comets in the cloud are frozen bodies a few kilometres across, like dirty snowballs. There are thought to be countless millions of them in the cloud, but at that great distance they are invisible from the Earth.

Occasionally, the gravity of a passing star nudges some of the dirty snowballs out of the cloud and towards the Sun. As they approach the Sun they start to warm up. The ice turns into gas, and dust is released. The gas and dust form a cloud called the *coma*, which can grow to become ten times the size of the Earth. At the centre of the coma lies the dirty snowball, termed the comet's *nucleus*.

Once the comet develops a coma it becomes big and bright enough to be seen in telescopes from the Earth. In some cases the gas and dust stream away to form a *tail*. A comet's tail can stretch for 10 to 100 times the distance from the Earth to the Moon. The tail is blown by the effects of sunlight and the solar wind so that it always points away from the Sun, no matter in which direction the comet is moving.

As a comet moves between the planets, its path can be altered by their gravitational pull so that it comes back to the Sun regularly. The comets with the shortest orbits probably come from the innermost part of the Oort Cloud, known as the *Kuiper Belt*.

Each year dozens of comets are seen through telescopes. Some are new discoveries while others are known comets returning to the Sun. The comet with the shortest orbit is Encke's Comet, which goes around

▲ **Comet Hale–Bopp,** a bright comet seen in 1997. The broad, white tail is made of dust, while the narrower blue tail is gas.

◄ **The nucleus of Halley's Comet,** as photographed by the Giotto space probe. The surface of the nucleus is dark, but bright jets of gas and dust are being squirted out to form the coma and tail.

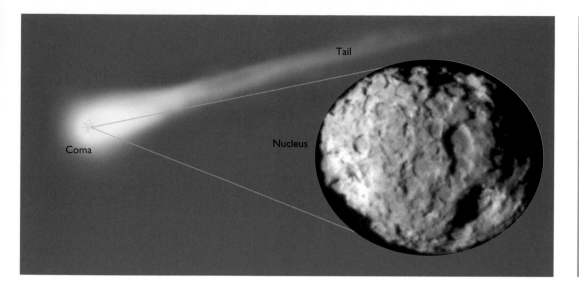

Tail

Coma

Nucleus

This stamp, issued in 1986 by Great Britain, shows Edmond Halley looking something like his comet.

▲ *The three main parts* of a comet: the coma, the nucleus and the tail. Together, the nucleus and coma form the head.

the Sun every 3.3 years. But other comets take over a million years to go around the Sun. Most comets are named after the people (or sometimes the spacecraft) who discover them. Many comets have been discovered by amateur astronomers who spend their nights looking for them.

Every so often a comet becomes bright enough to be seen with the naked eye and puts on a ghostly show in the night sky. In the past, people thought that comets were bad omens and they feared them. Although a comet looks impressive, particularly in photographs, it is mostly composed of gas far thinner than the Earth's atmosphere. A comet would be dangerous only if its nucleus actually hit us.

To find out more about what comets are made of, in 2004 a NASA probe called Stardust flew through the coma of the comet Wild 2. It collected dust samples, which it is due to bring back to the Earth for study in 2006. A European probe called Rosetta is due to catch up with a comet called Churyumov–Gerasimenko in 2014 and drop a lander onto its nucleus to analyse its composition. This will be the first-ever landing on a comet.

Halley's Comet

The most famous comet in history is named after an English astronomer, Edmond Halley, the first person to realize that comets orbit the Sun. In 1705 he suggested that the comets seen in 1531, 1607 and 1682 were all the same one, orbiting every 76 years or so. And he predicted that it would return again, around 1758. True enough, the comet did come back as predicted and it was named after him. Halley's Comet last appeared in 1986, when several

spacecraft were sent to meet it. The European space probe Giotto went right through the comet's head, passing 600 kilometres (375 miles) from the nucleus. It took photographs showing the comet's nucleus, which looks like a lumpy potato. The nucleus is about 16 kilometres (10 miles) long and is made of ice with a dark, dusty crust. This was the first time that a comet's nucleus had been seen. Halley's Comet is not due back again until 2062.

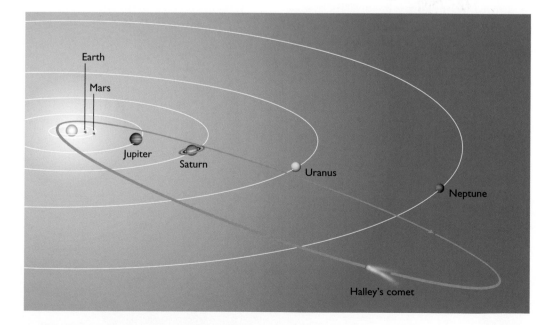

Earth

Mars

Jupiter

Saturn

Uranus

Neptune

Halley's comet

▲ *At its closest to the Sun,* Halley's Comet comes inside the orbit of Venus.

Its very elongated path takes it out beyond Neptune's orbit.

47

ASTEROIDS, THE COSMIC KILLERS

ASTEROIDS, also called minor planets, are rubble left over from the formation of the Solar System. The first asteroid was found by chance in 1801 and named Ceres. Now about 100,000 are known, ranging from blocks the size of a mountain up to Ceres, the largest, which is over a quarter the size of our Moon.

The brightest of them, Vesta, can sometimes be seen with the naked eye if you know exactly where to look, but the others are too faint to see without binoculars or a telescope.

Most asteroids orbit in a region called the asteroid belt, between Mars and Jupiter, but some stray through the inner Solar System. Learning more about such stray asteroids is important because, if one were found to be heading our way, we would need to divert or destroy it.

With this in mind, in February 2000 an American space probe called NEAR Shoemaker went into orbit around the asteroid Eros, studying its composition and sending back images of its rocks

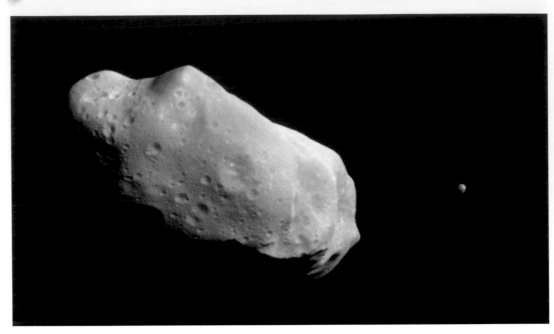

and craters. After a year in orbit, the probe descended to the surface to make its final measurements.

CERES DATA

DISTANCE FROM SUN:	414 million km
DIAMETER:	948 km
TIME TO ORBIT SUN:	4.6 years
TIME TO SPIN ON AXIS:	9 hr

▲ *The American space probe Galileo took this photograph of the asteroid Ida, which it passed on its way to Jupiter. Ida turned out to be a lump of rock about 55 kilometres (34 miles) long, pitted with craters. It has a tiny moon, Dactyl, seen on the right of the picture. Ida looks very much like the two moons of Mars, Phobos and Deimos, which are thought to be captured asteroids.*

Did an asteroid kill the dinosaurs?

About 65 million years ago, a major disaster struck the Earth. The dinosaurs, the most fearsome animals ever to roam our planet, mysteriously died out, and so did many other creatures. Scientists have found a strange layer of clay among the Earth's rocks that was formed at the time the dinosaurs died. The clay is unlike any other found here. Scientists think that this clay is made up of dust from a large asteroid that hit the Earth in the Yucatán peninsula of Mexico. The dust would have spread around the globe and changed the Earth's climate for years before finally falling to the ground. The dinosaurs could not survive in this new climate, and died out. If another large asteroid hit the Earth today, it might be humans that die out.

METEORS AND METEORITES

ON ANY clear night you may see a sudden streak of light, often called a *shooting star*. Actually, shooting stars have nothing to do with stars at all. They are caused by specks of dust burning up as they plunge at high speed into the Earth's atmosphere. The proper name is a *meteor*.

Strung out along the orbits of comets are streams of dust particles. Several times a year, the Earth passes through some of this dust, and a *meteor shower* is seen. During such a shower, dozens of meteors can be seen each hour, radiating from one part of the sky. A meteor shower can last several nights.

Occasionally, a far larger piece of Solar System debris enters the atmosphere and reaches the ground. This is known as a *meteorite*. Although the name is similar, meteorites are quite different from meteors. Most meteorites are chips off asteroids, although some have come from the surfaces of Mars or the Moon. Meteorites can be of rock or metal.

The atmosphere slows down small meteorites so that they fall harmlessly to the surface, but the largest ones are still moving very quickly when they hit the ground and they blast out a crater. Most of the craters on the Moon were caused by impacts from meteorites and asteroids. Scientists collect meteorites because they are free samples from other parts of the Solar System.

The world's largest known meteorite is made of iron and weighs about 60 tonnes. It fell in prehistoric times in Namibia, Africa, where it still lies.

▲ **Meteors belonging to a given shower** seem to come from the same point in the sky. This point is called the radiant of the shower. Here, members of a meteor shower streak away from their radiant, as seen over a period of an hour or more.

◀ **About 50,000 years ago** a meteorite weighing thousands of tonnes crashed into the Arizona desert in the United States. The hole it made is known as Meteor Crater (although really it should be Meteorite Crater), 1200 metres (4000 feet) across and 180 metres (600 feet) deep.

STARS AND CONSTELLATIONS

THE STARS may seem uncountable, but no more than about 2000 of them are visible to the naked eye on any clear night. In a town, you will be able to see just a few dozen of the brightest ones because of the glare from street lights. It is only when you look at the sky through binoculars or a telescope that the stars really do become impossible to count.

Stars seem to form patterns in the sky, called *constellations*. The Greeks and Romans of old named these star patterns after characters from their myths, which made the constellations easier to remember. We still use the old names today, as shown on the maps on the following eight pages.

More recently, astronomers have invented newer constellations for the stars in the southern skies. The Greeks and Romans could not see these stars because they never rose above the horizon in Greece and Italy. There are now 88 constellations, covering the whole sky. Although the stars of each constellation lie in the same direction in space, most of them are at vastly different distances from us. So there is no real connection between most of the stars in a constellation at all.

Star distances are often measured in *light years*, which is how far a beam of

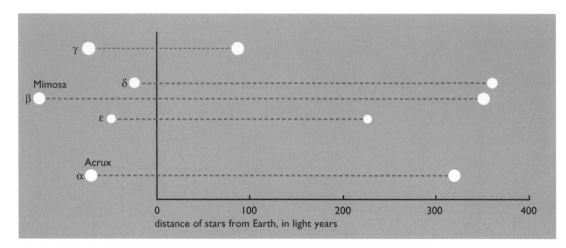

distance of stars from Earth, in light years

▲ **The constellation Crux,** the Southern Cross, is shown on the left as it appears to us. If we could travel hundreds of light years out into space and look at these five stars from a different direction, we would see that they lie at very different distances from Earth and do not form a true cross at all. If we lived on a planet orbiting a distant star, we would see different constellation patterns in the sky.

The smallest of the constellations is also one of the most famous – Crux, the Southern Cross. The ancient Greeks saw these stars as part of the legs of Centaurus, the centaur.

light travels in one year. Light moves at the fastest speed known, 300,000 kilometres (186,000 miles) per second. Therefore it takes light just over a second to reach us from the Moon, over 8 minutes to reach us from the Sun, and 4.3 years to reach us from the nearest star to the Sun, which is called Alpha Centauri and lies in the southern half of the sky. Many of the stars we see at night lie hundreds of light years away – in other words, their light has taken centuries to reach us.

How bright a star seems to be depends on both its actual brightness and how far away it is. For example, Sirius is the brightest star in the night sky. It gives out 20 times as much light as the Sun, but that alone does not account for its brightness at night. What is also important is that it is among the nearest stars to us, only 8.6 light years away. Some stars give out thousands of times more light than Sirius, but to us they appear fainter because they are much farther away.

The changing shapes of the constellations

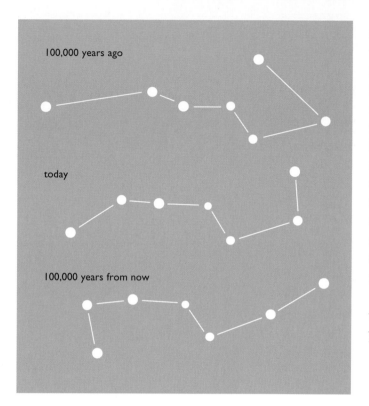

100,000 years ago

today

100,000 years from now

Stars are all moving through space at high speeds, but because they are so far away we do not notice any movement, even in a human lifetime. But over very long periods of time the shapes of the constellations will change. This diagram shows how the seven stars of the Plough have moved over the past 100,000 years, and how they will look 100,000 years from now.

◄ *Maps of the night sky* were once like this. As well as the stars themselves, they depicted the mythical characters, creatures, and objects after whom the ancient Greeks and Romans named the constellations. These two maps were made by the Dutch map-maker Andreas Cellarius in 1660. On the left are the constellations of the northern skies. The southern constellations are shown on the right-hand map.

If you compare these two old maps with the star charts on the following pages, you will find that the constellations are not all the same. Some we no longer use. For example, Cellarius drew Cancer Minor, the little crab, beside Cancer itself, but there is no such constellation now. Around the south celestial pole are some gaps which were filled in with new constellations about a hundred years after these maps were made. The large southern constellation Argo, the ship, at left of centre on the right-hand map, was later split into three: Carina, the keel, Puppis, the deck, and Vela, the sails.

STAR CHARTS

BETWEEN them, the star charts on the following pages cover the whole of the sky. The stars in the region around the north celestial pole are shown on these two pages. On pages 54–57 are charts of the sky either side of the celestial equator, and on pages 58–59 are the south polar stars.

When you look up at the night sky, the stars all seem to be on the inside of a huge dome. Although they really are not, this does give us a way of mapping the stars and describing their positions.

Maps of the Earth have a grid made up of lines of latitude and longitude. In their place, maps of the sky use lines of declination and right ascension. (These are marked on the charts as black dotted lines.) *Declination* is how far up or down a star is from the celestial equator. It is measured in degrees, from 0° at the equator to +90° (at the north celestial pole) or −90° (at the south celestial pole). *Right ascension* is how far around the sky the star is, and is measured from 0 to 24 hours. You will find these coordinates marked around the edges of the charts.

Brighter stars are shown on the charts as bigger spots. Astronomers use a scale of *magnitudes* to measure star brightnesses, and the key next to each chart gives the spot sizes for magnitude of 5.5 and brighter. Stars as faint as magnitude 6 or even 6.5 can be seen by people with good eyesight in very clear, dark skies, but they are not on these charts. A small number of other objects are shown, such as the Orion Nebula (see page 63), which lies close to the celestial equator.

A white dotted line winding across the four equatorial maps marks the *ecliptic*. This is the path the Sun appears to follow across the sky as the Earth goes around the Sun. The planets

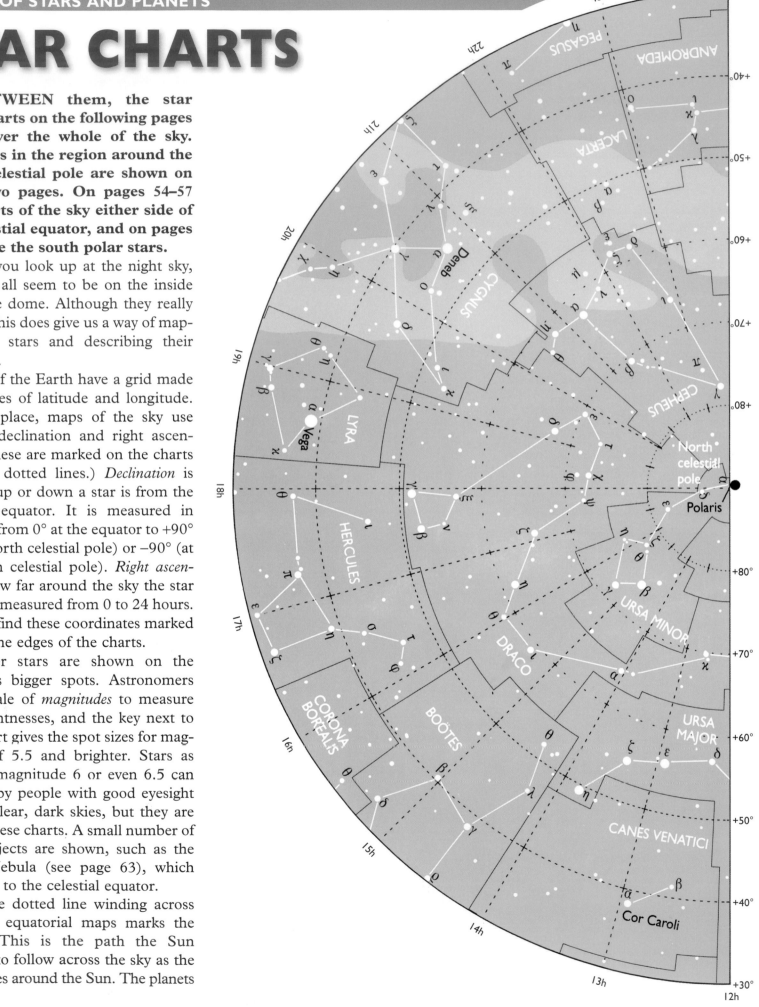

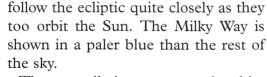

follow the ecliptic quite closely as they too orbit the Sun. The Milky Way is shown in a paler blue than the rest of the sky.

The constellation names are in white letters, and the boundaries between them are marked as black lines. Individual stars have names too, most of which came from the Arabic language. Only the names for the brightest stars are still in common use, and these are in black letters. Other naked-eye stars are identified by letters of the Greek alphabet. This scheme was introduced by Johann Bayer in 1603. In his star atlas he labelled the stars in each constellation in approximate order of brightness, starting with α (alpha), then β (beta), and so on. Here is the complete Greek alphabet:

α	alpha
β	beta
γ	gamma
δ	delta
ε	epsilon
ζ	zeta
η	eta
θ or ϑ	theta
ι	iota
κ	kappa
λ	lambda
μ	mu
ν	nu
ξ	xi
ο	omicron
π	pi
ρ	rho
σ	sigma
τ	tau
υ	upsilon
φ or ϕ	phi
χ	chi
ψ	psi
ω	omega

Key to star magnitudes

0 0.5 1.0 1.5 2.0 2.5 3.0 3.5 4.0 4.5 5.0 5.5

53

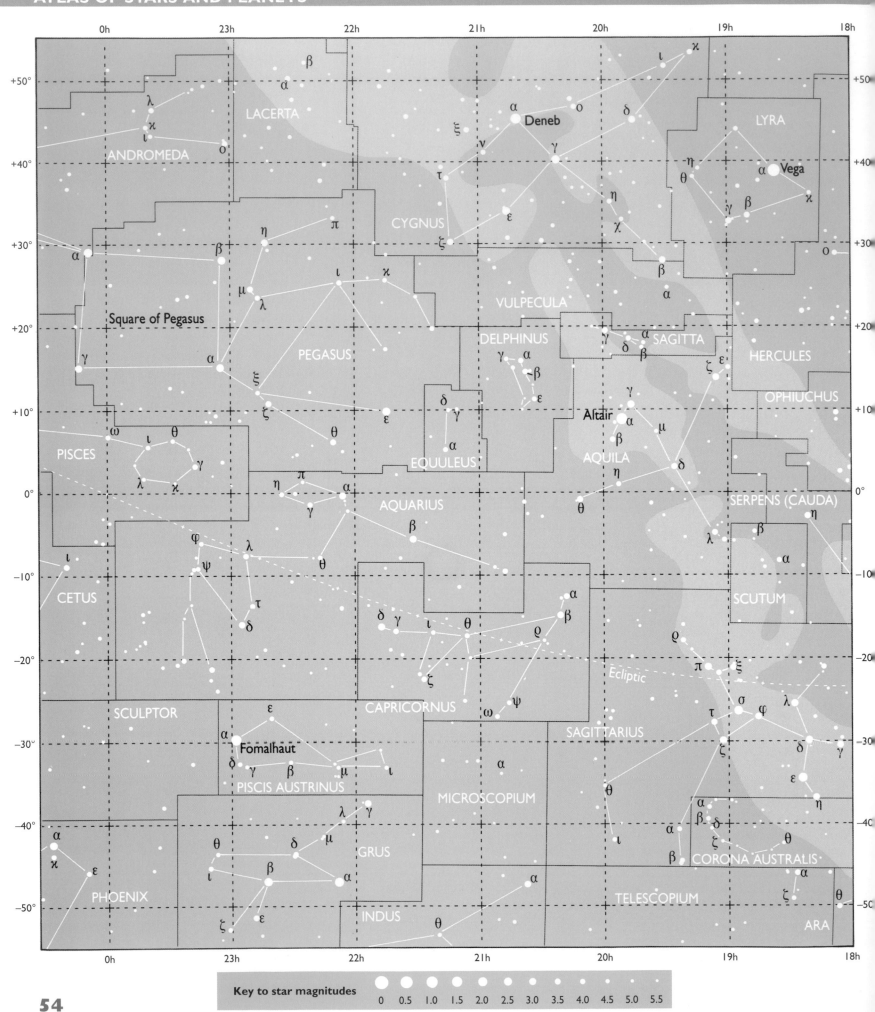

Key to star magnitudes

0   0.5   1.0   1.5   2.0   2.5   3.0   3.5   4.0   4.5   5.0   5.5

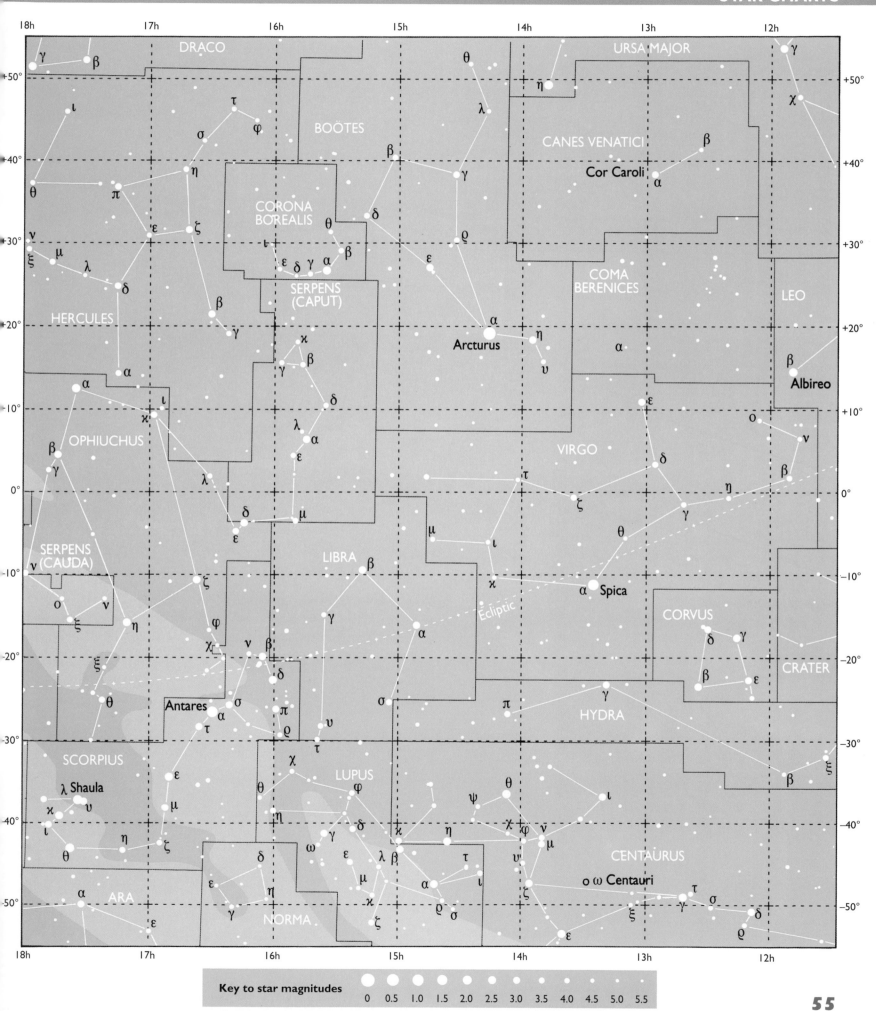

Key to star magnitudes

0   0.5   1.0   1.5   2.0   2.5   3.0   3.5   4.0   4.5   5.0   5.5

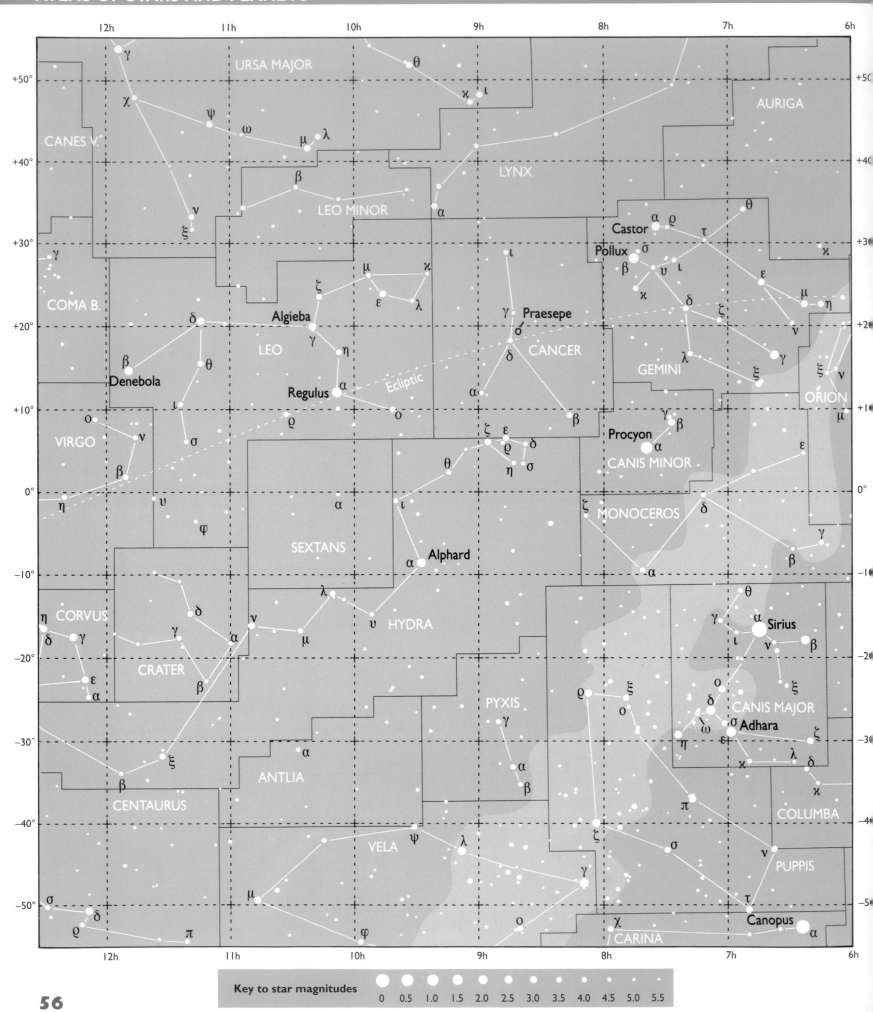

Key to star magnitudes

0 0.5 1.0 1.5 2.0 2.5 3.0 3.5 4.0 4.5 5.0 5.5

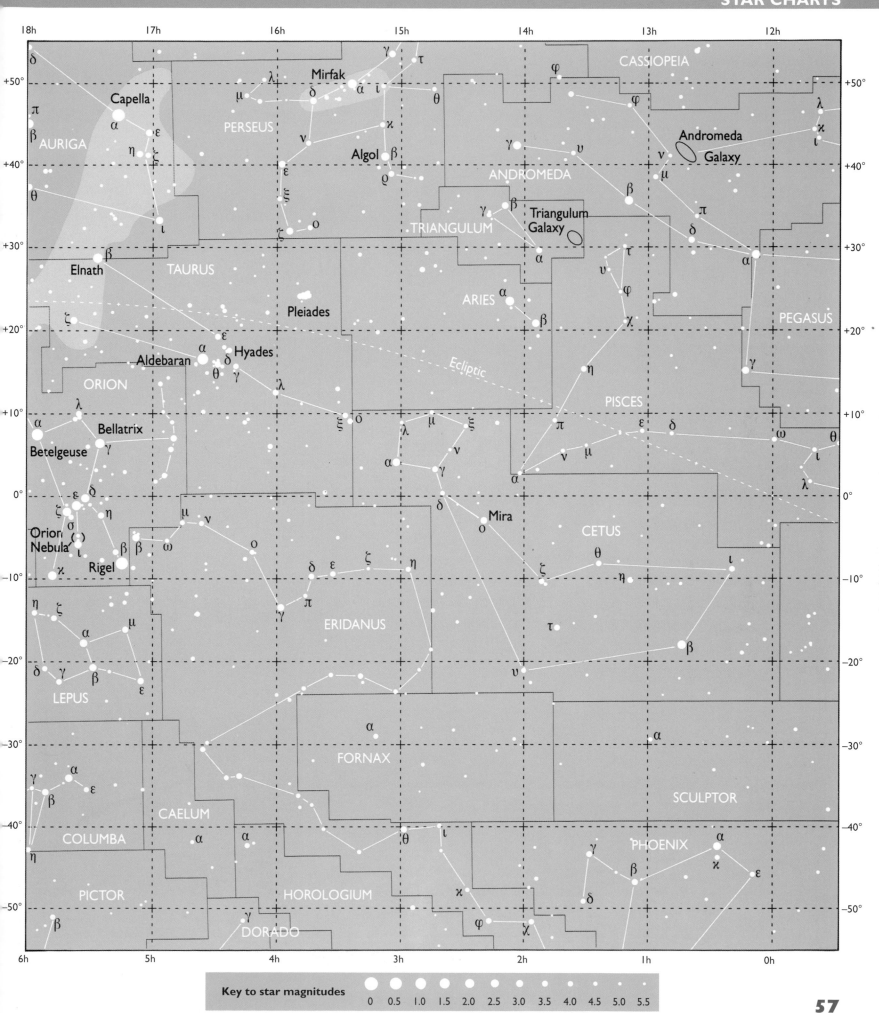

Key to star magnitudes

0 0.5 1.0 1.5 2.0 2.5 3.0 3.5 4.0 4.5 5.0 5.5

Constellation index

This index gives the page number of the main star chart(s) on which to find each of the 88 constellations.

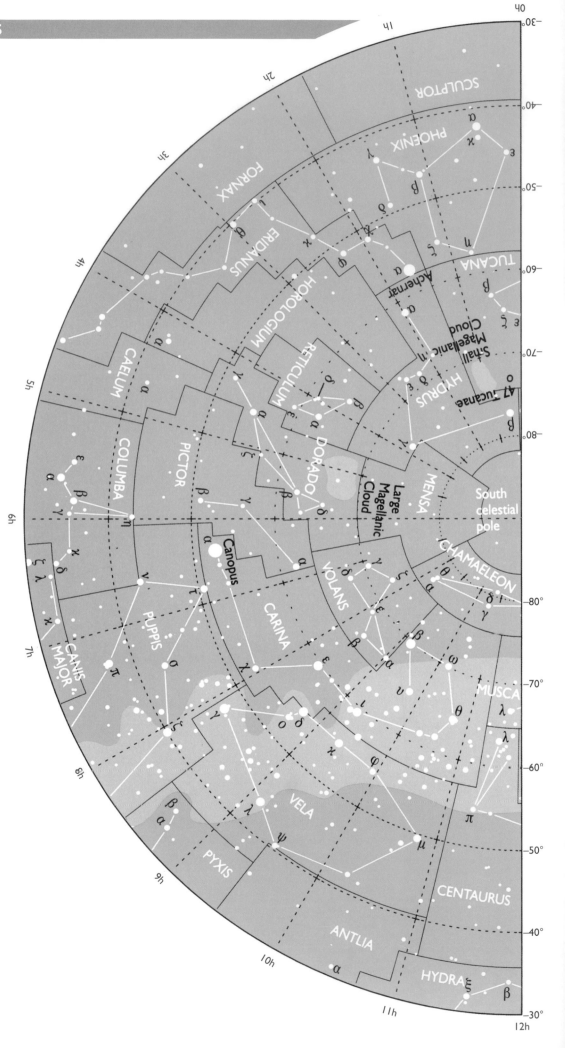

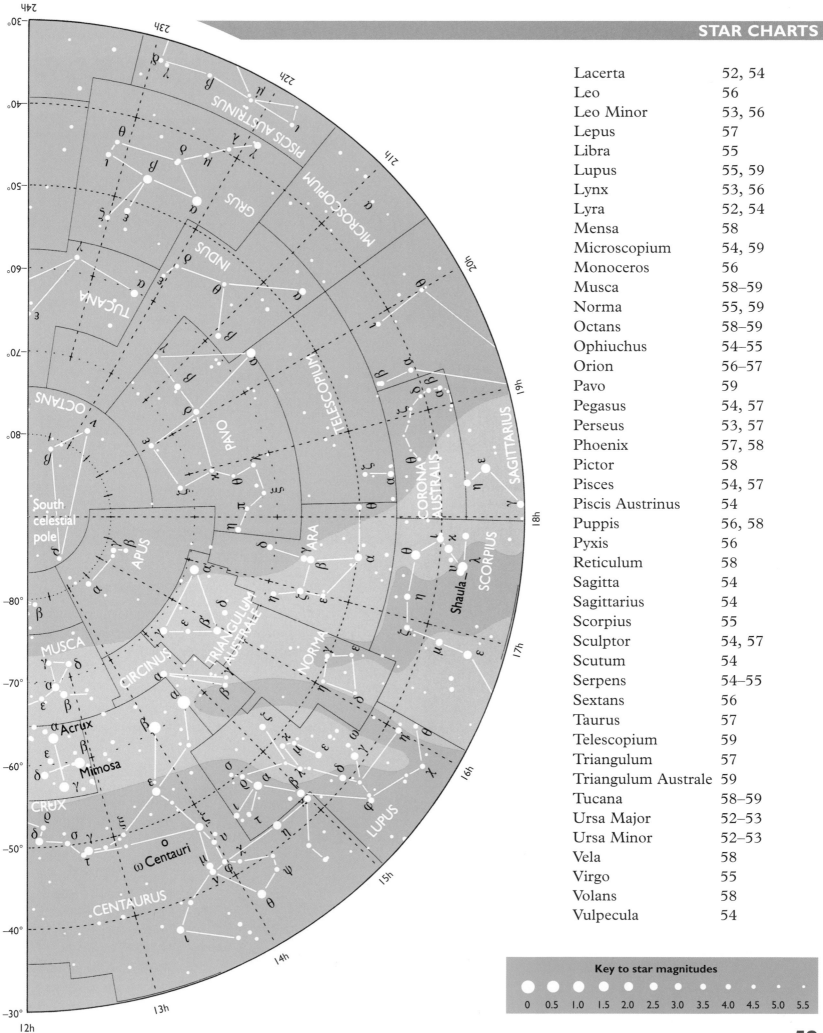

Key to star magnitudes

0   0.5   1.0   1.5   2.0   2.5   3.0   3.5   4.0   4.5   5.0   5.5

FINDING YOUR WAY BY THE STARS

BRIGHT stars and easy-to-spot constellations provide skymarks to help you find your way around the heavens. Find these stars and constellations on the maps on pages 52–59, and use them as signposts to other constellations nearby.

The stars on show at night will change from season to season as the Earth orbits the Sun. Also, which stars you can see depends on your latitude on Earth. And, of course, the night sky appears to spin round as the Earth rotates beneath it.

Finding north

The most familiar star group of all is the saucepan-shaped Plough or Big Dipper, actually part of the constellation Ursa Major (the Great Bear). Two stars of the saucepan's bowl point towards the north pole star, Polaris. In the opposite direction, these stars point to the constellation Leo, the lion. Following the handle of the saucepan takes you to Arcturus, the fourth-brightest star in the sky. If you have good eyesight, you will see that the second star in the handle of the saucepan has a twin. Binoculars show the two stars more clearly. The best time of year to see the stars in this diagram is in the spring.

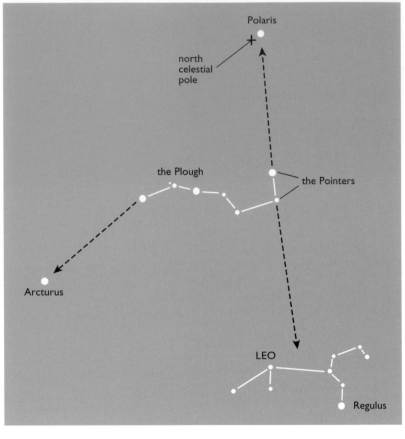

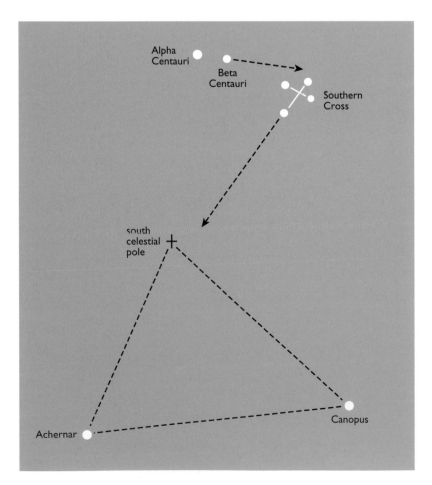

Finding the south pole

There is no bright pole star in the southern hemisphere. The Southern Cross, properly known as the constellation Crux, can be visualized as an arrow pointing to the south pole. The south pole of the sky forms a triangle with the bright stars Achernar and Canopus. Two other bright stars quite close together, Alpha and Beta Centauri, point to the Southern Cross. Alpha Centauri is the closest star to the Sun.

Sailors long ago used the stars to navigate at sea, as shown on this stamp from the Faroe Islands. Far away from the shore, with no landmarks to guide them, sailors took measurements of the stars at night to work out their position at sea. Great voyages of discovery were made possible by sailors' knowledge of the stars.

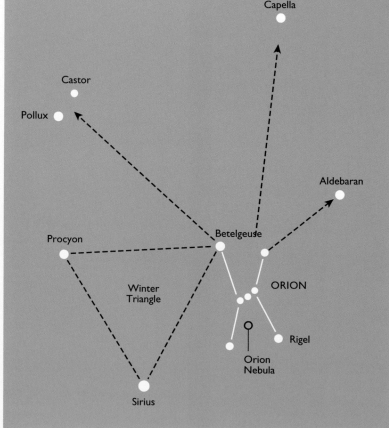

Stars in summer

In the northern hemisphere summer, three bright stars form a large triangle. They are called Deneb, Vega, and Altair. Vega is the brightest star in the constellation Lyra, the lyre. Deneb marks the tail of Cygnus, the swan. But the stars of the swan can just as easily be seen as a large cross. Sometimes, therefore, Cygnus is known as the Northern Cross.

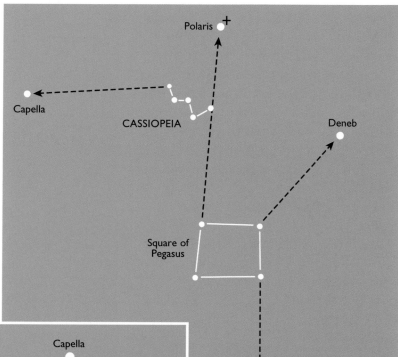

Stars in winter

In the south on northern winter evenings lies the magnificent constellation Orion, the hunter. The star at its top left, Betelgeuse, forms a large triangle with Sirius (the brightest star in the sky) and Procyon, another bright star. A line of three stars forms the belt of Orion. Below the belt is the famous Orion Nebula, a glowing cloud of gas just visible to the naked eye but more easily seen through binoculars. Above and to the left of Betelgeuse are two stars representing the celestial twins, Castor and Pollux. To the top right of Orion is Aldebaran, the brightest star in Taurus, the bull.

Stars in autumn

In the northern autumn sky lies the constellation Pegasus. Its main feature is a box of four stars, the Square of Pegasus. The square's sides can be used to locate Polaris, the north pole star, and a bright star in the south called Fomalhaut. Between Pegasus and Polaris is the constellation Cassiopeia. This is easy to recognize, because it is shaped like the letter W.

STARS AND STAR BIRTH

SPACE is mostly empty, but in places between the stars there are clouds of gas and dust called nebulae. Stars are born when gravity pulls the densest parts of a nebula into balls of gas. As the gas ball shrinks in size it gets so hot at its centre that nuclear reactions start (see pages 6–7), turning hydrogen into helium. These reactions give out light and heat, which is what makes the gas ball a true star. The Sun was born in this way 4600 million years ago. The planets grew from dust and gas that was left in orbit around it.

We can see the process of star birth in action today in places such as the Orion Nebula, a huge cloud of gas about 1400 light years from the Earth. New stars are being born here, and some of them have disks of gas and dust orbiting around them from which planetary systems are thought to be forming.

The biggest stars weigh as much as a hundred Suns and blaze millions of times more brightly than the Sun. At the other end of the scale, the smallest stars, known as red dwarfs, are mere glow-worms, one-tenth the size of the Sun and a thousand times fainter. Gas balls even smaller than red dwarfs never become hot enough at their centre for nuclear reactions to start. These are known as brown dwarfs, and they glow dimly before gradually fading away.

A star's lifetime depends on how quickly it uses up its hydrogen fuel. The Sun has been burning steadily for 4.6 billion years and is about halfway

▶ *An immense column of cool gas* in the Eagle Nebula, photographed by the Hubble Space Telescope. New stars are forming from knots of denser gas at the top of the column.

▶ **Stars are being born** in the Orion Nebula, a huge cloud of gas. This photograph, taken in infrared light, shows hundreds of young stars that have come into being from the nebula's gas within the past million years.

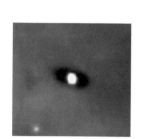

The Orion Nebula, a region where stars are forming, lies in the constellation of Orion, the hunter. It can be found to the south of a line of three stars which form Orion's belt, and is shown as a cluster of dots on this stamp from Botswana.

▲ **A dark disk of gas and dust** surrounds a young star in Orion. One day, a planetary system may form from this disk.

through its life. However, the biggest and brightest stars burn up their hydrogen far more quickly and run out of it in only a few million years, which is a fraction of the lifetime of the Sun. Red dwarfs, by contrast, burn so slowly that they can live for many times longer than the Sun.

When the hydrogen fuel in a star's core begins to run out, the star swells up in size. As it swells, the star's surface cools and turns redder. Such stars are called red giants. One day our Sun will become a red giant, a hundred times larger than it is at present. When that happens, about 5000 million years from now, the Earth will be roasted to a cinder.

▼ **This artist's impression** takes us 5000 million years into the future. The Sun is now a red giant, and we are looking at it from a burnt and lifeless Earth.

STAR DEATH

After a star like the Sun has swollen into a red giant, the outer layers drift off into space, like an enormous smoke ring. Such an object is termed a *planetary nebula* – not because it has anything to do with planets, but because some astronomers thought they looked like the rounded disks of distant planets when they were first seen through telescopes.

At the centre of a planetary nebula lies the small, hot core of the former star. Such a core is known as a *white dwarf*. A white dwarf star is about the size of the Earth, but weighs as much as the Sun. Because so much matter is squeezed into such a small ball, white dwarfs are very dense. A spoonful of white dwarf material would weigh as much as an elephant. Over billions of years, the white dwarf cools and fades out. Our Sun will end up like this.

The brightest and heaviest stars suffer a much more spectacular death than

▶ *This planetary nebula in the constellation Gemini is* popularly known *as the Eskimo Nebula because it looks like a face fringed by a fur parka. The picture was taken by the Hubble Space Telescope in 2000 and shows details that had never previously been seen.*

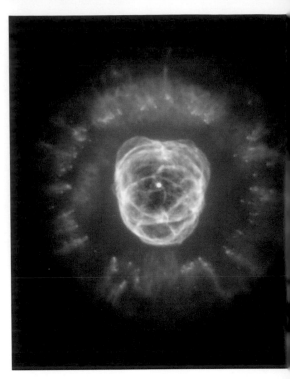

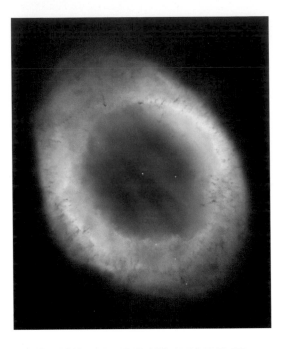

◀ *The famous Ring Nebula in the constellation Lyra, photographed here by the Hubble Space Telescope in 1998, is a beautiful example of a planetary nebula. The gas was thrown off by the faint star at the centre. The colours indicate different temperatures in the gas.*

Supernova 1987A

In 1987 astronomers in the southern hemisphere were lucky to see the first supernova bright enough to be visible with the naked eye for almost 400 years. It exploded into view in a small galaxy next to ours called the Large Magellanic Cloud. This photograph, taken in 1994 by the Hubble Space Telescope, shows red rings of gas thrown off by the star before it exploded. The remains of the exploded star lie at the centre of the middle ring. The supernova was so far away that the light from it took nearly 170,000 years to reach us. The other stars in the picture are not connected with the supernova.

ordinary ones. After swelling up into brilliant supergiants they blow themselves apart in a huge explosion known as a *supernova*. A supernova shines as brightly as millions of ordinary stars like the Sun for a few weeks or months, before it fades away.

The outer layers of the exploded star are blasted off into space at high speed. At the centre of the explosion something even stranger than a white dwarf is left behind. Often, the core of the star is squashed by the supernova explosion to form a *neutron star*. Such stars are only about 20 kilometres (12 miles) across, the size of a city.

Because neutron stars are so small, they can spin very quickly – many times a second. Every time they spin they give out a flash of energy, like a lighthouse. Usually this energy is in the form of radio waves, but sometimes it can also include light waves. A flashing neutron star is called a *pulsar*.

The matter in a neutron star is squeezed so incredibly tightly that a spoonful of it would weigh as much as a mountain. Its gravity is therefore

In 1572 a brilliant new star appeared in the constellation Cassiopeia, and was observed by the Danish astronomer Tycho Brahe. We now know that this star was a supernova. The remains of the exploded star can still be detected by astronomers. A plan of Tycho's observatory, one of his observing instruments and the location of the supernova are shown on this stamp from the island of Ascension.

The Crab Nebula

In the year 1054, people on the Earth saw a bright new star flare up for a few months in the constellation Taurus. The cause was a star that died in a supernova explosion. At the site of the explosion, the remains of the star that blew up can still be seen through telescopes: a vast expanse of glowing gas that is still expanding. It is called the Crab Nebula, because an astronomer in the nineteenth century thought it looked like a crab's claws. At the centre of the Crab Nebula is a pulsar that flashes 30 times a second. The sequence of photographs at left shows the pulsar's flash building up and then dying away.

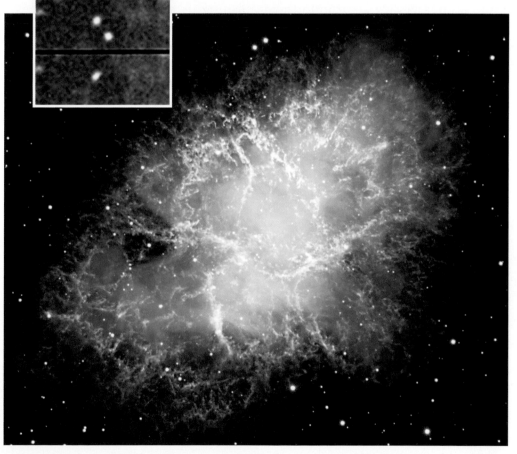

immensely strong. But if a neutron star contains more matter than about three Suns, its gravity becomes so strong that it shrinks even further, until it vanishes from sight. Such an object is called a *black hole*. At the centre of the black hole the star that died is crushed out of existence by the force of gravity.

Nothing can get out of a black hole, not even light. However, things can fall in, including gas from nearby stars, and this is how we can detect black holes. As gas swirls around the hole before falling out of sight, it heats up to many millions of degrees. Satellites in space have spotted a number of places where hot gas is believed to be falling into a black hole.

STAR FAMILIES

MOST stars are members of families – twins, triplets, or even larger groups. For example, through a telescope we can see that the closest star to the Sun, Alpha Centauri, is actually a pair of stars. They orbit around each other every 80 years. Many other stars that look single to the naked eye turn out to have one or more partners when seen through a telescope.

In some pairs, the stars pass in front of one another as they go around their orbits, which causes an eclipse. When this happens, the light from one star is blocked off and we see the star fade for a few hours or days. The star returns

▼ *The best-known star cluster,* the Pleiades, is about 400 light years away in the constellation Taurus. Its stars are immersed in a cloud of dust which gives the cluster a hazy appearance on photographs.

to its normal brightness when the eclipse ends.

Young stars are often found in bunches of dozens or hundreds, all of them born from the same cloud of gas. One of the most famous star clusters is the Pleiades in the constellation Taurus, the bull. If you have good eyesight you may be able to count six or more stars in the Pleiades. Binoculars reveal dozens of stars in the group. They all formed within the past 50 million years or so, which makes them young as stars go – the Pleiades did not exist when the dinosaurs were alive on the Earth, for example.

Taurus contains another famous star cluster, the Hyades. This group, shaped like the letter V, is much older than the Pleiades. Its brightest stars can be seen with the naked eye and the rest are easily seen in binoculars.

Such groups are called *open clusters* because the stars are usually widely

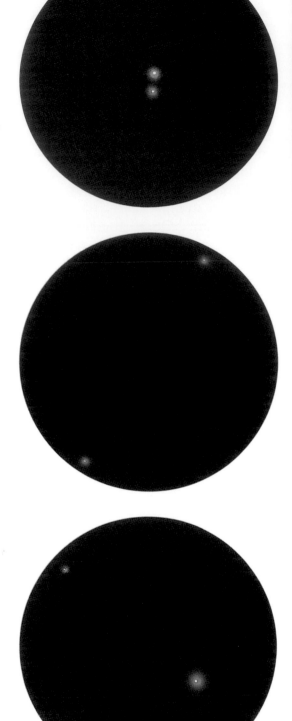

▲ *Seen through a telescope,* Alpha Centauri (top) is a pair of yellowish suns. Epsilon Lyrae (middle) is a group of four stars – two are far apart, but each has a closer companion. Albireo (bottom), in the constellation Cygnus, is made up of a yellow and a blue star. The colours of the stars indicate their temperatures. The reddest stars are the coolest, and the bluest the hottest.

▼ **If the orbit of a pair of stars** is lined up so as to be seen almost edge-on from Earth, they will pass in front of each other and the brightness will appear to change, especially when a large, dim star passes in front of a brighter companion. The most famous star of this type is Algol, in the constellation Perseus. During eclipses, which occur every three days, its brightness sinks to one-third its usual value.

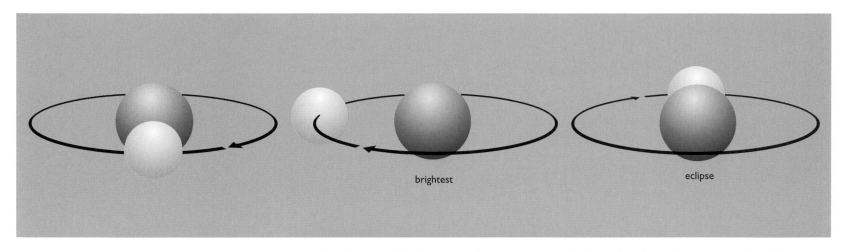

brightest

eclipse

Taurus, the bull, contains two famous clusters of stars. The V-shaped Hyades cluster forms the face of the bull, while the smaller Pleiades group lies on the bull's back. The brightest star in Taurus is Aldebaran, a red giant which marks one of the bull's eyes.

scattered. But there is another type of star group that contains hundreds of thousands of very old stars much more densely packed than in open clusters. These groups are rounded in shape and are called *globular clusters*. The stars in them are over twice as old as the Sun. They were among the first stars to have formed in our Galaxy.

▲ **M3 is a large globular cluster** containing hundreds of thousands of stars. This photograph of its crowded central region was taken with a large telescope in Arizona. The brightest stars are red giants, seen scattered around the cluster.

OUR GALAXY

OUR SUN and the stars that make up the constellations are all part of a huge grouping called the Galaxy. From our position inside the Galaxy it is difficult to see what it looks like. But astronomers have worked out that its shape is a huge spiral, rather like a coil of rope.

The Galaxy is over 100,000 light years wide, which means that a beam of light (or a radio signal) would take more than 100,000 years to cross it. Our Sun lies in one of the spiral-shaped arms of the Galaxy, about halfway from the middle of the Galaxy to its rim, so we are in the suburbs. Beyond the edge of our Galaxy is empty space, and then other galaxies. (Our Galaxy is written with a capital letter G.)

On a clear night you can see the distant stars in our Galaxy. They form a faint band of light across the sky, the Milky Way. If you look at the Milky Way with binoculars or a telescope, you will see that it is made up of stars crowded together in their thousands. Our Galaxy itself is sometimes called the Milky Way.

There are about 250,000 million stars in the Galaxy. This is only a rough guess, for no one has counted them all. If you tried counting them at the rate of 100 a minute, without stopping, it would take you nearly 5000 years.

As well as middle-aged stars like the Sun, the spiral arms of the Galaxy contain young stars in open clusters, and gas clouds (nebulae) where more stars are still forming. Dotted around the Galaxy are globular clusters, full of old stars. Old stars are also found in the centre of the Galaxy, which lies in the constellation Sagittarius.

The whole Galaxy is rotating. As with the planets of the Solar System, the stars nearest the centre go around quickest and those farthest away take the longest. The Sun goes around the Galaxy in about 220 million years. It has completed only about 21 orbits since it was born.

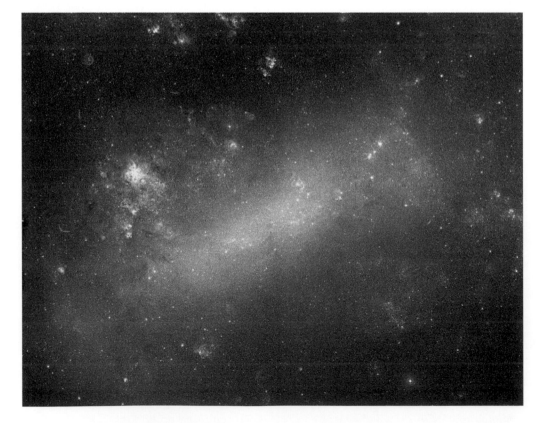

The Magellanic Clouds

Our Galaxy has two small neighbours. They both lie in the southern half of the sky and look like separate parts of the Milky Way. They are the Magellanic Clouds, named after the 16th-century Portuguese explorer Ferdinand Magellan, who saw them on his voyages around the world. The Large Magellanic Cloud is about one-tenth the size of our Galaxy and lies about 160,000 light years away. The Small Magellanic Cloud is smaller and more distant. Both are irregular in shape. This photograph shows the Large Magellanic Cloud. The pink patches are nebulae (gas clouds) where stars are forming. The biggest such area, called the Tarantula Nebula because it looks like a large tarantula spider, is 30 times the size of the Orion Nebula in our Galaxy.

▲ **This artist's impression** shows how our Galaxy might look from the outside. The Sun lies about halfway to the rim, in one of the arms that spiral out from the hub. Globular clusters are scattered in a halo around the centre of the Galaxy.

▼ **Towards the centre of the Galaxy,** the stars of the Milky Way crowd closely together. The stars at the very centre are normally hidden from view by thick clouds of dust. At infrared wavelengths, however, we can see through the dust to the core of the Galaxy, 25,000 light years away, which is at upper left in this image.

▲ **The beautiful Lagoon Nebula** is an area of star formation in a neighbouring spiral arm of our Galaxy, about 5000 light years from the arm in which our Sun lies. Star-forming clouds such as this are dotted along the arms of all spiral galaxies.

The centre of our Galaxy lies in the southern constellation Sagittarius, the archer, where the stars of the Milky Way crowd together.

69

GALAXIES AND THE UNIVERSE

Our Galaxy is one of countless galaxies dotted throughout the Universe, like islands in a vast ocean. Galaxies come in three main shapes. Many of them are *spirals*, like our own Galaxy, in which stars and gas clouds lie in arms that curl out from the hub. A sub-division of the spiral galaxies are the *barred spirals*. These have a bar of stars across their centre, and the spiral arms start from the ends of the bar. In common with many spirals, our own Galaxy has a trace of a bar at its centre.

Totally different are *elliptical galaxies*. These have no arms at all – instead, they are rounded in shape. Elliptical galaxies come in a wide range of sizes. The largest ellipticals contain over ten times as many stars as the Milky Way and are the biggest galaxies known. But the smallest elliptical galaxies are just like large globular clusters.

Some galaxies have no particular shape at all, and are known as *irregulars*. The two Magellanic Clouds that accompany our Galaxy are examples.

Most galaxies belong to clusters. Our own Galaxy is the second-largest member of the Local Group, which contains about three dozen galaxies. The largest member of the Local Group is a spiral galaxy in the constellation Andromeda. It can just be seen with the naked eye on clear nights as a fuzzy patch, and is easily found in binoculars.

The Andromeda spiral galaxy is a slightly larger version of our own Galaxy. It lies about 2.5 million light years away, which means that the light from it now reaching us left there while ape-men lived on the Earth. The Andromeda spiral galaxy is the most distant object that we can see with the naked eye, without binoculars, or a telescope.

▼ **The Andromeda spiral galaxy** is *much like our own, but about twice as big. It too has two small galaxies as companions. They are visible in this photograph, one above it and one below.*

▲ *The Sombrero Galaxy is a spiral galaxy seen almost edge-on. It has a large, bright centre crossed by dark lanes of dust in its spiral arms, giving it a resemblance to a broad-brimmed Mexican hat.*

▲ *A barred spiral galaxy, known as NGC 1300. (Most galaxies are known by numbers given to them in lists drawn up by astronomers of the past.) Barred spirals have two curved arms that emerge from the ends of a straight central bar.*

The spiral galaxy NGC 2997, shown on an Australian stamp. The galaxy was photographed through the Anglo-Australian Telescope, which is in New South Wales, Australia.

Interacting galaxies

Most galaxies lie far apart, but sometimes one may may pass close to another and may even collide with it. One famous example of a galaxy being disturbed by a passer-by is the Whirlpool (right), a beautiful spiral with a smaller companion. The smaller galaxy is actually in orbit around the Whirlpool, and the two probably brushed past each other millions of years ago. In another pair, called the Mice (bottom), two spiral galaxies of similar size have passed close to each other, and gravity has pulled out long streams of stars and gas, like the tail of a mouse. The two will eventually merge to form a large elliptical galaxy.

Most remarkable of all is Centaurus A (left), an elliptical galaxy with a band of dust wrapped around it. Astronomers think that Centaurus A's unusual appearance results from the merger of an elliptical galaxy with a spiral galaxy.

THE ORIGIN OF THE UNIVERSE

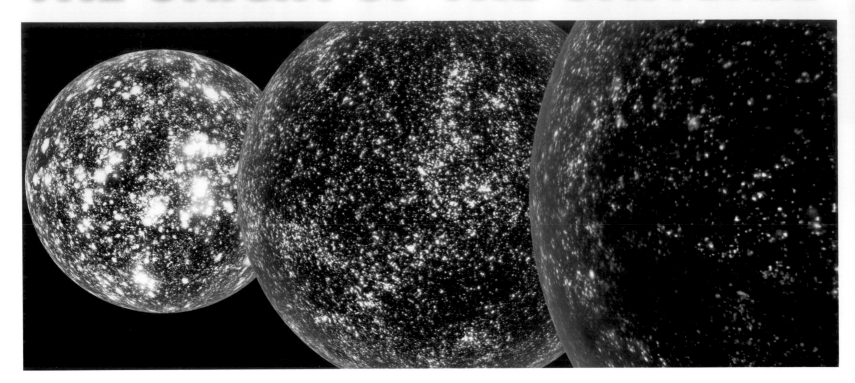

I N THE 1920s, an American astronomer named Edwin Hubble made a sensational discovery: the Universe is getting bigger. He found this out by studying galaxies far off in space through the 2.5-metre (100-inch) telescope on Mount Wilson in California. At that time it was the biggest telescope in the world.

As Hubble looked farther and farther into the depths of space, he noticed that galaxies appeared to be moving apart. In other words, the entire Universe must be swelling up rather like a balloon.

This is an important clue to how the Universe began. Astronomers now think that the entire Universe was once contained in a single, super-dense blob. For some unknown reason, the blob exploded. This explosion is known as the Big Bang. The galaxies

are the bits from that explosion, still flying outwards as the space between them expands.

From the speed at which the galaxies are moving, we can work out how long ago the Big Bang happened. The answer is over 13,000 million years ago, roughly three times the age of the Sun and the Earth.

At the time of the Big Bang, the temperature of the Universe was many millions of degrees. It has since cooled to only 3°C above the coldest temper-

▲ **The Big Bang** started the Universe expanding over 13,000 million years ago. The Universe is still expanding, and as it does so the countless galaxies within it are all moving apart from one another.

ature possible, absolute zero. Absolute zero is −273°C, so the temperature of the Universe is −270°C. One of the major areas of astronomical research is the study of the earliest stages of the Universe through large telescopes on Earth and in space.

▶ **Quasars** observed by the Hubble Space Telescope. The one at right lies at the core of an elliptical galaxy, while that at far right has been caught merging with a galaxy.

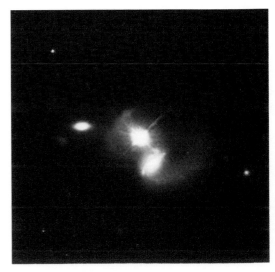

Looking back in time

Large telescopes can detect objects so far away that their light started out on its journey to us long before the Earth was born. Therefore, by looking far into space we can look back in time, to see how the Universe appeared in the distant past. When the Universe was still young it contained many ultra-bright objects called *quasars*. A typical quasar is a hundred times brighter than our Galaxy but only a few times the size of our Solar System. How can something so bright be so small? Quasars are thought to be young galaxies with huge black holes at their centres, swallowing gas and stars. As the gas swirls around the black hole before plunging in, it gets hot and shines brightly. Similar events are happening in what are called *Seyfert galaxies*, which are spirals with unusually bright centres.

▼ *Galaxies extend as far* as the largest telescopes can see. This image of the far-off Universe taken by the Hubble Space Telescope captures the faintest and most distant objects ever seen, showing how the Universe appeared when it was still young.

In 1965 two Americans, Arno Penzias and Robert Wilson, discovered that empty space is not entirely cold. It has a temperature of 3 degrees above absolute zero, due to heat left over from the Big Bang. In 1978 Penzias and Wilson received a Nobel prize for their discovery, as commemorated on this stamp from Sweden, the country that awards the Nobel prizes.

▶ *A Seyfert galaxy,* a type of spiral galaxy with a brilliant centre. A quasar might look like this if seen close-up.

◀ *Slight variations in temperature* of the Big Bang show up as different colours in this map made by a space satellite. The temperature differences marked the places where the first galaxies began to form.

TELESCOPES AND BINOCULARS

TELESCOPES show objects that are too faint to be seen with the naked eye, and they also make them appear closer. To do these two seemingly magical tricks, they collect light rays into an image (picture) of the object and then enlarge it.

One type of telescope has a lens at the front end of its tube. This is known as a *refracting* telescope. The lens refracts (bends) the incoming light to form an image. A smaller lens, called the eyepiece, magnifies (enlarges) the image so that the object appears closer. For example, through a telescope with an eyepiece that magnifies 100 times, we would seem to hover 4000 kilometres (2400 miles) above the Moon's surface.

In *reflecting* telescopes, a curved mirror at the bottom of the telescope tube bounces light into the eyepiece via a smaller second mirror. Some telescopes use both lenses and mirrors, but it is

Binoculars

Binoculars are like two small telescopes joined together, so that you can look through them with both eyes. They are smaller and easier to carry than a telescope and are good for simple star-spotting. Light passing through binoculars is 'folded' by two wedges of glass called prisms, which is why binoculars are shorter

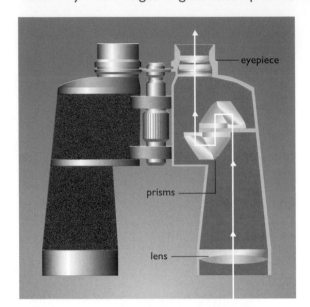

than telescopes. Binoculars carry markings such as 8 × 40 or 10 × 50. The first figure is the magnification, and the second is the size of the front lenses in millimetres. Binoculars usually magnify between 6 and 10 times and have front lenses from 30 mm to 50 mm wide. Binoculars give beautiful wide-angle views of the sky. They are useful for sweeping over the star fields of the Milky Way, looking at large star clusters, observing comets, and picking out stars and nebulae that are too faint for the naked eye.

always the size of the main lens or mirror that is the most important. Larger lenses and mirrors show fainter objects and smaller details because they collect more light. The most powerful telescopes can see objects 10 million times too faint for the naked eye.

Big mirrors are cheaper and easier to make than big lenses, so all large telescopes are reflecting ones. Very large mirrors are now being made from many smaller pieces fitted together. Two major examples are the twin Keck Telescopes, which have mirrors 10 metres (33 feet) wide made from 36 pieces of glass. They are on a high mountain called Mauna Kea in Hawaii, where the skies are particularly clear.

The world's largest refractor, at Yerkes Observatory in the United States, has a lens 1 metre (40 inches) across and was built as long ago as 1897. It is still used for research.

▲ *A night-time observing session.* The instrument being used is a 150-millimetre (6-inch) reflector, a popular choice for amateur astronomers. It is important to keep warm while observing, so be sure to wrap up well when going out of doors.

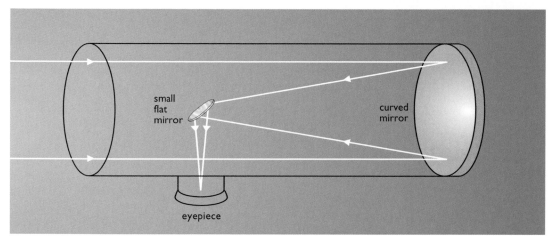

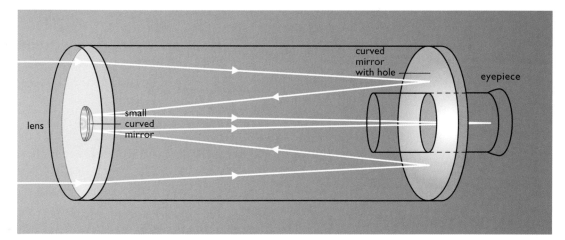

◄ **These diagrams** show how the three main types of telescope work. At the top is a refractor, which focuses light with a lens. The middle diagram shows a reflector, which uses a curved mirror instead of a lens. The telescope at the bottom uses mirrors and a lens to bring light to a focus. All telescopes have a lens for an eyepiece.

In 1990 the Hubble Space Telescope was launched into orbit by the Space Shuttle. It has a mirror 2.4 metres (94 inches) wide, but it can see the sky more clearly than smaller telescopes on the ground because it is above the Earth's atmosphere.

How to observe

People are often disappointed with their first view through a telescope. But with care and practice, your observing will be rewarding. First, even if you are only intending to look at the sky with the naked eye, find somewhere safe to observe that is away from the glare of artificial lights. Your eyes will need several minutes to get used to seeing faint objects in the dark, so be patient. Astronomers need to 'train' their eyes – the more observing you do, the more detail you will see in each object. Keep notes of your observations: what you have seen, the instrument used, and the date and time.

One important point to remember is that you must never look directly at the Sun through binoculars or a telescope. It is so hot and bright that it will damage your eyes in an instant.

▲ **The twin Keck telescopes** sit next to each other on a mountain top in Hawaii. They each have mirrors 10 metres (33 feet) across. The telescopes can be seen through the openings in their domes.

SEEING THE INVISIBLE

OBJECTS in the Universe do not just give out light that we can see. They also give out a whole range of other waves, from radio waves (the longest) to X-rays and gamma rays (the shortest), which we cannot see. However, these waves can be picked up by special instruments on Earth and in space.

Radio waves are collected by radio telescopes, which are usually in the form of large metal dishes rather like reflecting telescopes. Radio telescopes are very much larger than optical telescopes because radio waves are much longer than light waves. The largest radio astronomy dish is 305 metres (1000 feet) wide, at Arecibo in Puerto Rico. Often, many smaller radio telescopes are linked together to give a more detailed picture of the sky than one single dish could produce alone.

Radio waves and some infrared waves get through the atmosphere. Most other waves do not, and so they have to be studied from space. Different types of wave are given out by different types of object. For example, infrared rays are a good way of studying cool stars and

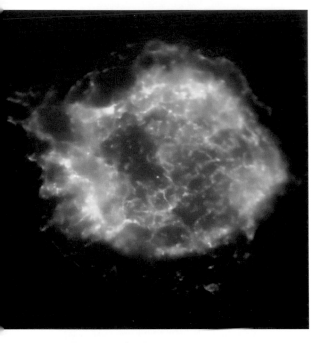

◀ **An expanding cloud of gas** in the constellation Cassiopeia, in an image taken by the Chandra X-ray Observatory. The gas was thrown off by a star that exploded as a supernova about 350 years ago. Different colours are a key to the temperature and composition of the gas.

▶ **The peculiar galaxy Centaurus A** observed at several wavelengths. Plots of X-ray (blue) and radio (pink and green) emissions, overlain on an optical image, show jets of hot gas being shot out from the galaxy's turbulent core.

clouds of gas in space. Orbiting telescopes have studied star birth at infrared wavelengths and found signs of planetary systems forming around nearby stars.

Very hot gas gives out the shortest wavelengths – ultraviolet, X-rays and gamma rays. Some of the most exciting discoveries have come from X-ray satellites, which have found places in space where gas at temperatures of millions of degrees seems to be swirling around enormous black holes.

◀ **The Very Large Array** is a group of 27 radio telescopes in New Mexico in the United States. Each dish is 25 metres (82 feet) across and can be moved along rails 21 kilometres (13 miles) long in a Y-shape.

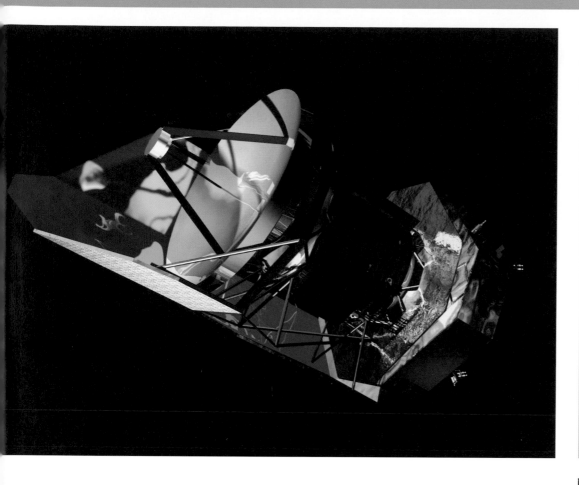

◀ **Herschel, a European Space Agency infrared observatory,** is due for launch in 2007 carrying a telescope 3.5 metres (138 inches) wide, the largest ever sent into space.

The world's largest radio telescope is at Arecibo, in Puerto Rico. It is 305 metres (1000 feet) across, so large that it cannot be steered. Instead, it scans the sky above it as the Earth rotates.

The spectrum

Light has a range of colours from blue to red, as in a rainbow. This band of colours is known as the *spectrum*. The colour of light depends on the length of the waves that make it up. Blue light has the shortest wavelength and red light the longest. Beyond the blue and red ends of the spectrum are other wavelengths we cannot see. Ultraviolet waves (also known as UV) are shorter than blue light. Shorter still are X-rays and gamma rays. These short wavelengths can be detected only by instruments in space, since they do not get through the Earth's atmosphere. At the other end of the spectrum, infrared rays are longer than red light. Longest of all are radio waves, which are picked up by radio telescopes. All these waves travel at the same speed – the speed of light, 300,000 kilometres (186,000 miles) per second, the fastest speed in the Universe.

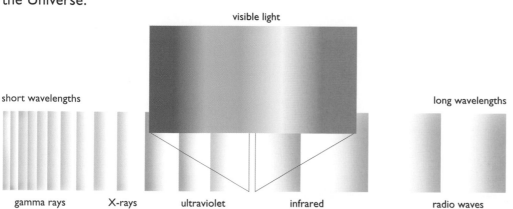

visible light

short wavelengths

long wavelengths

gamma rays   X-rays   ultraviolet   infrared   radio waves

▲ **The Andromeda spiral galaxy** seen at ultraviolet wavelengths by NASA's Galex (Galaxy Evolution Explorer) spacecraft. The image shows blue regions of young, hot, high-mass stars tracing out the spiral arms where star formation is occurring, and the central orange-white bulge of old, cooler stars.

QUIZ QUIZ QUIZ QUIZ QUIZ

1. Which is the largest planet in the Solar System?
2. Which is the third planet from the Sun?
3. Which planet comes closest to Earth?
4. How many kilometres are we from the Sun, roughly?
5. Which gas is the main component of the Sun and other stars?
6. What is the nuclear process called that powers the Sun and stars?
7. Who was the first person to walk on the Moon?
8. Which planet is known as the Red Planet?
9. Which planet has a Great Red Spot?
10. Which planet is tilted on its side?
11. Where in the Solar System would you find the Ocean of Storms?
12. Where in the Solar System would you find Olympus Mons?
13. Where in the Solar System would you find Cassini's Division?
14. What are the names of the two small moons of Mars?

15. Which is the only moon in the Solar System with thick clouds?
16. What is the name of Jupiter's volcanically active moon?
17. Which American space probe flew past the planets Jupiter, Saturn, Uranus and Neptune?
18. Who discovered the planet Pluto?
19. What is the name of the European space probe that is due to land on a comet in 2014?
20. What is the cloud of comets at the edge of the Solar System called?
21. Which is the closest star to the Sun?
22. How many light years away is the closest star to the Sun, roughly?
23. How many constellations are there in all?
24. Which is the smallest constellation?
25. Which constellation is pictured as a bull?
26. Which constellation is pictured as a lion?
27. Which constellation represents a swan?
28. Which is the brightest star in the night sky?

29. What is the name of the north pole star?
30. What is the name given to a cloud of gas from which stars form?
31. What is the name given to the explosion of a big star at the end of its life?
32. What type of star will be left when the Sun dies?
33. What is the distance in light years from one side of our Galaxy to the other, roughly?
34. What shape is our Galaxy?
35. What are the two small companion galaxies of our Galaxy called?
36. Who discovered that the Universe is expanding?
37. What is the name given to the event which is thought to have started the expansion of the Universe?
38. What is the speed of light in kilometres per second, roughly?
39. Are the largest optical telescopes reflectors or refractors?
40. Where is the world's largest radio telescope, 305 m wide?

Answers on page 80

CREDITS

(*t* top, *b* bottom, *l* left, *r* right, *c* centre)
Star charts on pages 52–59 prepared from computer plots and Milky Way outlines by Richard Monkhouse.
Illustrations © Philip's
Julian Baum: 5*t*, 17*t*, 24*cl*, 33*b*, 44, 48*b*, 49*cr*, 63*b*, 66*r*, 68–69*t*, 72*t*.
Raymond Turvey: 4–5*c*, 7*cr*, 7*br*, 13*b*, 17*b*, 20*b*, 21*t*, 25*b*, 47*tl*, 47*b*, 50*t*, 51*t*, 60–61, 67*t*, 74*t*, 75*t*, 77*b*.
Stamps from author's collection.
Photographs
Dr. R. Albrecht, ESA/ESO Space Telescope European Coordinating Facility; NASA: 45*c*.
© Anglo–Australian Observatory/Royal Observatory, Edinburgh. Photograph by David Malin: 68*b*.
HJP Arnold/Sol Invictus: 16*tl*, 16*tc*, 16*tr*, 20*t*, 21*tl*.
John Bahcall (Institute for Advanced Study, Princeton) Mike Disney (Univ. of Wales) and NASA: 72*bc*, 72*br*.
Reta Beebe (New Mexico State Univ.), D. Gilmore, L. Bergeron (STScI), and NASA: 37*br*.
Photographs courtesy of EFDA-JET: 7*bl*, 7*bc*.
ESA/DLR/FU Berlin (G. Neukum): 31*cl*.
P. Challis (Harvard-Smithsonian Center for Astrophysics): 64*b*.
Akira Fujii/David Malin Images: 46*t*.

ESO: 65*cr*, 71*c*.
ESA. Illustration by Medialab: 77*tl*.
Rob Gendler: 66.
Calvin J. Hamilton: 25*t*, 35*br*, 41*tl*, 41*tr*, 43 *tc*.
Jeff Hester and Paul Scowen (Arizona State Univ.), and NASA: 62.
HST Comet Team and NASA: 33*tc*, 33*cr*.
Hubble Heritage Team (AURA/STScI/NASA/ESA): 64*c*.
Bill Hutchinson/Galaxy: 13*cr*.
S. Kafka and K. Honeycutt, Indiana Univ./WIYN/NOAO/NSF: 67*br*.
Erich Karkoschka (Univ. of Arizona) and NASA: 40*c*.
© UC Regents/Lick Observatory: 18*r*, 19*l*.
Lowell Observatory: 45*bl*, *br*.
Mark McCaughrean and ESO: 63*tc*.
Mark McCaughrean (Max-Planck-Institute for Astronomy), C. Robert O'Dell (Rice Univ.), and NASA: 63*cl*.
Hillary Mathis/NOAO/AURA/NSF: 71*cl*.
Max-Planck-Institut für Aeronomie: 46*b*.
Image by Craig Mayhew and Robert Simmon, NASA GSFC. Based on data from the Defense Meteorological Satellite Program: 14–15.
2MASS/G. Kopan, R. Hurt: 69*r*.
NASA: 9*br*, 10*t*, 10*b*, 16*b*, 19*tr*.
NASA Goddard Space Flight Center: 11*t*.
NASA Johnson Space Center: 11*bl*.
NASA, ESA, JPL and the Hubble Space Telescope: 1, 4–5.

NASA/JPL/US Geological Survey: 22, 37 *bl*.
NASA/JPL/Northwestern Univ.: 23*cl*, 23*tr*.
NASA/JPL: 2, 26, 27*b*, 31*br*, 33*b*, 34, 35*c*, 35*bl*, 36*b*, 37*tl*, 37*cl*, 37*tc*, 38*tc*, 38*bl*, 38*br*, 39, 40*t*, 40*b*, 41*tcl*, 41*tcr*, 41*c*, 41*b*, 42, 43*tl*, 43*tr*, 43*bl*, 48*t*.
NASA/JPL/Cornell Univ.: 28.
NASA, J. Bell (Cornell U.) and M. Wolff (SSI): 29*cl*.
NASA/US Geological Survey: 29*r*, 30*c*, 31*t*.
NASA Goddard Space Flight Center/MOLA Science Team: 30*b*, 31*bl*.
NASA/JPL/Univ. of Arizona: 32, 33*tl*, 43*br*.
NASA and The Hubble Heritage Team (STScI/AURA):36*t*.
NASA/JPL/Space Science Institute: 38*tr*.
NASA, Andrew Fruchter and the ERO Team [Sylvia Baggett (STScI), Richard Hook (ST-ECF), Zoltan Levay (STScI)]: 64*r*.
NASA/ESA and The Hubble Heritage Team (STScI/AURA): 71*tl*.
NASA, Holland Ford (JHU), the ACS Science Team and ESA: 71*br*.
NASA, ESA, S. Beckwith (STScI) and the HUDF team: 73*tr*.
NASA/WMAP Science Team: 73*bl*.
NASA/CXC/SAO: 76*tl*.
X-ray (NASA/CXC/M. Karovska et al.); Radio 21-cm image (NRAO/VLA/J. Van Gorkom/Schminovich et al.), Radio continuum image (NRAO/VLA/J. Condon et al.); Optical (Digitized Sky Survey UK Schmidt

Image/STScI): 76*tr*.
NASA/JPL/California Institute of Technology: 77*br*.
NOAO/AURA/NSF: 69*b*, 73*br*.
Novosti: 24*b*.
Image courtesy of NRAO/AUI: 76*b*.
David Parker/Science Photo Library: 49*b*.
Pekka Parviainen: 7*t*, 12*t*.
Philip Perkins: 70*b*, 71*tr*.
T.A. Rector (NOAO/AURA/NSF) and Hubble Heritage Team (STScI/AURA/NASA): front endpaper
T. Rector/Univ. of Alaska Anchorage and WIYN/NOAO/AURA/NSF: back endpaper
Royal Astronomical Society: 50–51*b*.
Royal Swedish Academy of Sciences: 9*tl*.
Robin Scagell/Galaxy: 13*tc*, 74*b*.
N.A. Sharp/NOAO/AURA/NSF: 65*t*.
Peter H. Smith and Mark Lemmon of the UA Lunar and Planetary Laboratory, and NASA: 37*tr*.
SOHO (ESA & NASA): 8*t*, 8*b*.
SOHO/MDI research group, Stanford Univ.: 9*tr*.
SOHO (ESA & NASA): 23*b*.
Alan Stern (Southwest Research Institute), Marc Buie (Lowell Observatory), NASA and ESA: 45*r*.
A. Tayfun Oner: 27*t*.
Tourism Canada: 21*bc*, *br*.
US Geological Survey/Clementine: 18*cl*.
Richard J. Wainscoat/Galaxy: 75*br*.

INDEX

QUIZ ANSWERS

1. Jupiter.
2. The Earth.
3. Venus.
4. 150 million.
5. Hydrogen.
6. Fusion.
7. Neil Armstrong.
8. Mars.
9. Jupiter.
10. Uranus.
11. The Moon.
12. Mars.

13. Saturn's rings.
14. Phobos and Deimos.
15. Titan.
16. Io.
17. Voyager 2.
18. Clyde Tombaugh.
19. Rosetta.
20. Oort Cloud.
21. Alpha Centauri.
22. 4.3 light years.
23. 88.
24. Crux, the Southern Cross.
25. Taurus.
26. Leo.

27. Cygnus.
28. Sirius.
29. Polaris.
30. Nebula.
31. Supernova.
32. White dwarf.
33. 100,000 light years.
34. Spiral.
35. The Magellanic Clouds.
36. Edwin Hubble.
37. Big Bang.
38. 300,000 kilometres per second.
39. Reflectors.
40. Arecibo, Puerto Rico.

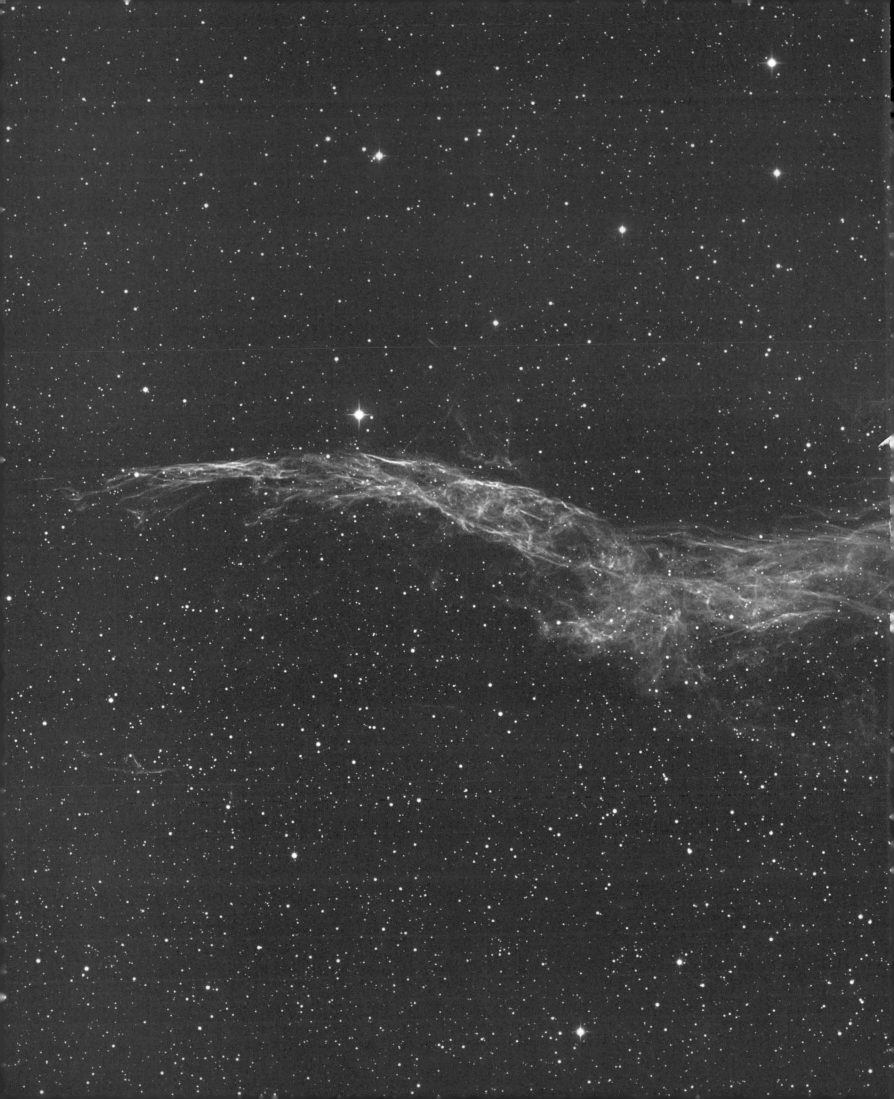